Time Under the Cross

Surrendering to the Will of God

Ron C. Enderle

PublishAmerica
Baltimore

First printing

PublishAmerica has allowed this work to remain exactly as the author intended, verbatim, without editorial input.

Hardcover 978-1-4512-9180-3
Softcover 978-1-4489-4848-2
PUBLISHED BY PUBLISHAMERICA, LLLP
www.publishamerica.com
Baltimore

Printed in the United States of America

"There are stages in the spiritual life of every man, where he must carry his Cross. Only then, is he ready to go where Our Lord wishes."
—*Prof. Plinio Correa de Oliveira*
Founder, Society for the Defense of
Tradition, Family and Property (TFP)

Dedicated to St. Jude the Apostle, My Confirmation Saint

Blessed St. Jude, help that I be ever mindful of the many lost and suffering souls in this world. Please ask God to grant favor to each as He has for me so many times through your intercession and by the intercession of the entire communion of Saints. I will always honor you as my special and powerful patron, and I will forever encourage grateful devotion to you. Amen

Foreword

For the majority of the past fifty years I have walked through life with a stride that is quick paced and one that is extremely focused in terms of my chosen path and the means to how and where I would arrive. However, I always seem to be in constant battle with an internal obstacle that never tires at planting seeds of doubt, despair and denial along the way. By the grace of God, my stride tends to place me steps ahead of this obstacle and typically I am successful at maneuvering out of its planned diversions and destructive intent.

Being raised Roman Catholic in a city with the honored name of Corpus Christi (Body of Christ), myself and my four siblings were nurtured by loving parents, our own and countless other parents of our life long neighborhood friends. We were schooled in the Catholic faith by dedicated stewards though I do recall times when I felt as if my faith was being administered in a manner that seemed as being very repetitive and some what robotic.

When I turned the age of twelve, my three older brothers were diagnosed with a rare heart disease. Though my younger sister and I did not have the disease, we were not immune to the emotional trauma and spiritual healing this trial would have on our family.

Literally over night these three young men, in their teens, began to encounter adult sized emotions and decisions, under the care of our parents, which would leave indelible marks on many of the mile stones throughout my life and the lives of others as well.

My father, now deceased, was a strapping gentleman from San Antonio, Texas with drive and charisma that was, for me, the personification of what every Christian man should strive to become. With great pride, I admit that I continue to emulate my Dad every day.

My mother, still with us as I write, is a striking lady, also from San Antonio, who most people generally admire for her beauty, both inner beauty and outer beauty. Many of these same people have known me for years and when I am present, they just love to add; "obviously your Mom's charm and looks skipped you and graced your sister instead." Mom armed our family with her profound faith while lovingly supporting Dad's lead without being overly submissive, in a negative light. My prayer life and my softer side, when evident, are attributed to Mom.

Though marred with sin just like each and everyone else, the compilation of my parent's individual and collective (one in the eyes of God) qualities are what defines me, and for this I am forever grateful. Thank you Mom and Dad.

All events in each of our lives are treasured moments. There are just some events that many of us wish to leave buried. This book, I pray, will inch all of us a little closer to having a better appreciation for the Divine and eternal importance of each event or mile stone in our life; whether large or small, joyful or immensely painful. I prepared this work of love as a tribute to our Heavenly Father for the many gifts bestowed upon me and my loving wife, Crickett, and our three daughters; Shea, Randi and Sami. The gifts I speak of are both tangible and intangible. I also thank God for those situations we do not have in our lives; i.e., a broken home, incurable disease, a luke warm faith, etc.

My saving grace throughout this opportunity to serve God has come namely from intense prayer, by many, and the utmost of confidence that the Holy Spirit would guide and protect despite the efforts of the enemy to disillusion me along the way.

In preparation of this book I kept hearing from my heart; "listen for and build around a theme that sums up the resounding message or 'quiet whisper' from God that has been your strength during your **time under the Cross**." I now understand that my time under the Cross was not just the time(s) when I felt most defeated or separated from the right to feel joy. I now understand that "time under the Cross" is all times. Though the severity of pain and joy may fluctuate "the Cross" is ours to carry out of love for Christ who carried the Cross because of my/our sins though He was without sin. To really appreciate the price He paid for us and to joyfully accept the Cross during good times and not so good times we must surrender our control and faithfully listen for and serve God.

The central theme of this book is simply this:

Surrenderment is a continuous process. It requires an enduring faith, a mature sense of purpose and the determined will to forgo the lures and direct assault from evil in our midst while we quest for eternal life with God the Father.

I close the Forward segment of this book with the prayer I wrote following many discussions with others about this undertaking. Though I have many others I do acknowledge as having prayed with me and counseled me, I do wish to recognize one dear friend, Phyllis Nesloney, who had to nearly hit me over the head with God's road sign before I truly heard the calling to pursue this labor of love.

Prayer

Lord, please be with me always, especially as I step out and discern over the prospect of writing a book that, through Your will, has a Word spreading value and results in the saving of many souls, including my own.

You created me in Your image and I wish to use this venue to help broadcast Your promise of eternity made possible by the life, death and resurrection of Your only Son, Jesus.

May the Holy Spirit guide my motives throughout this process. May our Blessed Mother Mary, in union with all Saints, pray with me and for me as I set self aside and placed salvation in my sights.

Heavenly Father I ask that You allow my Confirmation Saint, St. Jude, your servant Job and the late Deacon Auburn to walk with me through this work of love—this account of trials, triumphs and surrender being prepared in Your honor and for Your glory.

In Your Son Jesus' name I pray. Amen.

Acknowledgments

Those listed below, in addition to my Mom, my Dad and Phyllis Nesloney; mentioned in the Forward, are a small sampling of so many loving people who have made such a positive impact in my life. Their selfless acts of prayer, kindness and generosity were extremely instrumental in me being open to and able to serve God through this inspired writing.

Sr. Angela—Your tireless and no bars held stewardship throughout my spiritual journey has and will continue to bare much fruit. God gifted you with talents you so fearlessly use to lift others. Thanks for the lift.

Janet Lee—The "J" in your first name will always remind me of the Joy you bring into the lives of others. You have shown me, by example, how to rejoice even in the time of pain and misfortune.

Larry Grove—The song "Were You There" posses several questions about Jesus' Passion. You have shared with me several trials in your life where Jesus allowed you to experience His Passion in many respects. You were "there" and you endured the pain, accepted His grace and now so poetically share your gift of humble prayer with all who God sends your way.

Rick and Margie Svetlik—Crickett and I have been humbled by your Christian Action throughout the years. You both have a spiritually mature understanding of the message Jesus was sending when He first washed the feet of the Apostles. Our gratitude for your loving support is immeasurable as is God's rewards in Heaven for all who love and serve with great compassion.

Msgr. Seamus McGowan—You were the celebrant at Crickett's and my Wedding and you have remained in our lives and have helped so many to see Christ through your loving and caring demeanor as a servant of God. Much of what I cover in this writing was in part inspired by your own words and actions throughout our long friendship.

Eugene DeBoise—Though we only spoke on three occasions and for a short period each time, you encouraged me with your conviction and certainty that God will provide and that we should all give praise to Him through Jesus Christ our Lord and Savior. Thank you for allowing God's light to shine through you.

Paul Demzik—I grew up in the business world with you and I am also proud to say we have grown up in our shared faith together as well. Your positive attitude in every situation is infectious and has helped me through some pretty tough times. Now days when I get dragged through the dirt, I just apply your outlook and thank God for the pocket full of free topsoil.

John and Cathy Ell—For many years you both have been our neighbors across the street who never tired at greeting, listening to and comforting each and every member of our family. Thank you for the living, or should I say loving, example of doing what Jesus commands of us all; "you shall love your neighbor as yourself."

The Auburn Family—Thank you for supporting Deacon Auburn in his vocation to serve God in the Catholic Church. I am certain the good Deacon has been praying with me during my writings. May he rest in peace and may the perpetual light of Christ shine upon him. Amen.

Shea, Randi and Sami—God blessed your Mom and me with three beautiful and spiritual daughters. We love each of you dearly and we give thanks to God always for the privilege to have you in our lives. Thank you for your prayers and your patience as I was tucked away at times during my writing of this book. Now, will somebody please clean the cat box.

Crickett—You always say; "we make good decisions." Our decision to remain open to God's will throughout the years has been one of the best decisions ever. I love and respect you beyond description and I thank God for you everyday.

Part I
SURRENDERMENT

Chapter One
THY WILL BE DONE

"If I surrender, I will have given up all that I have worked for, all that I have anguished over, all that I have dreamed to achieve." This "I" laden quote is from me. It is something that resonated in the hustle and bustle of my mind every time others would speak of the concept of surrenderment. Some would refer to it as "letting go and letting God" or "a leap of faith." Others would say things such as "It is time to give the helm over to the real Captain" and one my Dad often said of himself; "Well, it was His to begin with and God knows I've done all I can to screw it up."

The fact that I once referred to "surrendering" as a concept shows how shallow and undeveloped my faith was at the time. Though my life has been well rooted in a Catholic Christian belief system, many times over I have hit what I felt was rock bottom. Each event or series of events would test my level of mental and spiritual maturity, or the lack thereof, and I would submit to the opposing force, the bottom made of rock, verses submitting or surrendering to "The Rock" who has no bottom and who is, above all, God. "The Lord is my rock."1

Throughout the Bible, God the Father has many endearing names; The Rock, Creator, Lord of Lords, King of Kings, Jesus, Savior, Friend, etc. In the book of Matthew and the book of Luke, our Friend and Savior, Jesus, tells us how to pray. In particular, He says; "Thy will be done."2 This portion of what is reverently referred to as "The Lord's Prayer" or "The Our Father" is a positive affirmation. A sublime and supreme promise, God's will, is going to take place, His will *is* going to happen, it *shall* be done. Jesus is telling us here that we must always have the mindset that what is coming, "Thy Kingdom," is true and definite. Jesus is telling us to continually transform our thoughts and our actions so that we can be found worthy to reside with Him in Heaven for eternity.

As mentioned in the "Forward," when I was twelve years old, my three brothers were diagnosed with a rare heart disease. Over the course of the next thirty years, each would eventually die as a result of the disease. My eldest brother was the first to be diagnosed and he, at the young age of eighteen, had to immediately deal with his mortality, straight on, due to the severity of his condition. The night before my brother, and our parents, left for Houston, Texas where he would have open heart surgery, he sat with our family and slowly recited "The Our Father."

My brother meticulously took each stanza and after saying it, he would, in his own words, tell us what Jesus' Word meant to him. I recall how he explained "Thy Will be done" to us in a soft tone and with a slow delivery that, surprisingly, had a calming affect as we listened in awe. He spoke of God having planned things out in such a way that though we might not quite understand it now, we would really enjoy it later. He talked about how we as a family needed to not be let down by future events and despite the outcome of his surgery we must stay true to God and prepare ourselves so that we can be together forever in Heaven.

Roughly seventy two hours after my brother concluded his rendition of "The Lord's Prayer," I found myself alone in the corner at a family friend's home where my younger sister and I were staying while our parents were away. I was praying as hard as I could and asking God to not take my brother. My brother had made it through surgery but his kidneys were not functioning well and he was now near death. Moments later, our friends rushed us to our home where our other two brothers were staying and we awaited "the call" from our Dad.

I hit rock bottom for the first time in my life when my third oldest brother handed me the phone. My world, where I was part of a well rooted Christian family and where "all was well," was now upside down and sure to never correct itself much less be the same again. Of course, our Mom and Dad continued to assure us that with God our family would make it through this and we would become stronger as a result. For me, I just kept remembering that twelve year old boy afraid and alone in the corner of a small bathroom asking God, the Creator, to not let his big brother die.

As inhabitants of this earth, we are a product of many things, namely the environment we are reared within. I am not speaking of environment in the context of one living along the Battert rocks of the Baden region of Germany, the desolate Serengeti Plains of the Tanzanian Republic of Africa nor the rustic South Texas Gulf Coast region of the United States. As vast and remotely different each of these areas are in terms of geographic environment, the environment I am referring to is much more complex and much more dynamic than these pins in the map. The environment we are raised in consists of the multitude of experiences and choices we are confronted with throughout our lives and even before birth, despite where we might live. There is the baby born to a mother addicted to cocaine who struggles through life with physical ailments resulting from her mother's addiction. There is the diabetic amputee who at age 40 looses a leg but not his dream to someday walk tall with a prosthetic replacement. And there is the young married couple starting their family while immersed in faith, hope and love.

Despite how different we all are and how fervent the enemy's attempts are to block us from all that is good, we must never forget that we have a common thread. Each and every one of us was made in God's image and each was given dominion over all other creation. *"God created man in His image; in the divine image He created him; male and female He created them. God blessed them, saying: 'Be fertile and multiply; fill the earth and subdue it. Have dominion over the fish of the sea, the birds of the air, and all the living things that move on the earth'."* **3** Though altered by the lure and corruption of sin, throughout time we have remained blessed by God and forever we are to be known as being created "in the Divine image" of the same and all powerful Creator. This blessed appointment, if you will, carries with it the awesome responsibility to live in and perpetuate the Divine love of God.

So, here we are, at the dawn of the 21st Century. Most people, throughout the world, are very much accustomed to the advances of technology and likewise are comforted by the same. Many of us have protected freedoms that are as accessible to us as the air we breathe. We wake each morning and navigate our way into the next day with little effort and at times little to no attention toward this process (to live in and perpetuate the Divine love of God) which is our awesome responsibility and privilege to partake of.

Now, are we, as creatures of God with "dominion over all living things…on the earth," living up to our awesome responsibility and are we truly reflecting "His image? I'm not. At least not always. Why? Because I too am a sinner and I allow the affects of my environment to convolute the true desires of my heart, which for me are best summed up in what Christ asked of us in the book of Matthew; "You shall love the Lord, your God, with all your heart, with all your soul, and with all your mind…you shall love your neighbor as yourself."4 If you are like me, then you may sometimes feel that you have, to some degree, already surrendered; surrendered to the pleasures or comforts of your environment and you find it rather difficult to justify change. I mean, come on, we go to Church; we slip the needy person a dollar or two when caught at the red light. We provide for our family, obey the laws; all while we try to make our mark in this world in such a way that makes us feel important while hopefully adding value to the next generation.

Surrenderment or the act of surrender in the context of doing God's will is not a catch phrase or a resolution. It is not making an occasional change in hopes to appease someone or something. It is a means to achieve an eternal end. I know, I just used an oxymoron—my apologies to all my English teachers throughout the years. "End" in this setting is meant as an objective. Though we are on this earth today, if we long to live eternally, we must remove our personal wants from the equation and rely on God's promise while we faithfully take action that mirrors His image and advocates our eternal end.

References to God's promise are mentioned throughout the Bible but one that speaks to me is from the book of James; "Blessed is a man who perseveres under trial; for once he has been approved, he will *receive the crown of life* which the Lord has promised to those who love Him."5

To mirror His image, we need to have knowledge of Him. The truest resource of this knowledge is through "the Word" and is found; you got it, in the Bible. Whether you are driven to thumb through it, study it along with a structured guide, or read it cover to cover, the Bible is "the Word" and "the Word" is the truth and as written in the book of John, "…and the truth shall set you free."6

My childhood was packed full of knowledge that came from the Bible, but not so much from our family reading or studying it per say. Each day at St. Theresa parochial school, Sr. Claude and other dedicated stewards would teach us kids Bible based curriculum, Baltimore Catechism at the time. My parents would teach and pray the Rosary 7 with us (each decade or mystery depicting blessed events found in the New Testament). Fellow Christian neighbors of various faiths would occasionally gather at our home and amongst the some twenty different conversations happening all at one time, scripture was some times an item of discussion. This diverse and continuous knowledge of the Word was and remains an essential benchmark for me as I attempt to mirror God throughout my life.

Case in point. Let's go back to my third oldest brother handing me the phone and my Dad telling me what the glistening eyes of my two brothers had already communicated. To not have had a base load of religious knowledge, even at the age of twelve, could have proven devastating in years to come. Without knowing who God is, why Jesus died for us, what is expected in the Commandments and what "Thy Will Be Done" means, I might have never lifted myself from that rock bottom and resumed a life as God intended.

Yes, life is riddled with the occasional pitfall, yet we can live one filled with opportunities to add to our knowledge and understanding of the Word. We can choose to spend our lives trying to emulate Christ at and after each turn and to rid ourselves of selfish tendencies. If we choose to, we can surrender to God and live with the commitment that "Thy Will Be Done."

Chapter Two
KNOWLEDGE

Surrenderment is a continuous process and to keep this process flowing there must be a timely infusion of diverse and accurate knowledge to complement the acknowledgement of and the commitment to God's will. In the previous chapter we touched on the need for knowledge in order to successfully surrender to God while increasing love and service for Him along the way.

This chapter will expand on what "knowledge," religious knowledge, really is and how it can be sourced via methods and means that stimulate your intellect while challenging your comfort level. Additionally, we will spend some time addressing the importance of getting to know God, through Jesus, and how to ask for wisdom as you become more knowledgeable and as you continue to surrender out of love for Him.

As previously mentioned, the truest resource of religious knowledge is available for us all in the Holy Bible, despite our preference of religion. God wanted everyone, throughout time, to know of His immeasurable and unconditional love for them. God, being Almighty, Wisdom itself, knowing of our human limitations, sent a variety of Prophets throughout the ages who told and foretold of His love and His Omnipotence. These messages, also consisting of His promises and His commandments, were echoed by the Prophets and other believers of the same Truth. Inspired accounts of each were documented for the benefit of all believers, for many generations to come, generations who would long to know of God so they too could honor and serve Him while passing this knowledge on to their children and their children's children.

The word "knowledge" has several definitions.

"The obtaining and recall of information"—Bloom's Taxonomy[1]

"Meaningful links people make in their minds between information and its application in action in a specific setting."—Nancy Dixon, author of Common Knowledge.[2]

"A fluid mix of framed experience, values, contextual information and expert insight that provides a framework for evaluating and incorporating new experiences and information."—Davenport and Prusak, authors of Knowledge Management.[3]

"The fact or condition of knowing something with familiarity gained through experience or association."—Merriam—Webster

In the Old Testament of the Bible, "knowledge"/"know," from the Hebrew root "yada" is intended to have a broader meaning than our English word "know."[4] It includes perceiving, learning, understanding, willingness, performing and experiencing. Knowledge is not the possession of information, but rather its exercise or actualization. To know is not to be intellectually informed about some abstract principle. God is not simply an intellectual apprehension. To know Him is to acknowledge and experience His reality. Because God's Word became Flesh as promised, the New Testament adds, and repeats throughout the Gospels, that "knowing" is a response of faith and the acceptance of Christ.

A spiritual song writer by the name of Judson W. Van DeVenter, wrote a song in the late 1800's titled "I Surrender All. **5** The first and last verse of Mr. Van Deventer's song speaks volumes of what is expected of us and is in store for us as we surrender to God and prepare for our eternity.

First Verse

"All to Jesus, I surrender; All to Him I freely give; I will ever love and trust Him, In His presence daily I shall live."

Last Verse

"All to Jesus I surrender; Now I feel the sacred flame. O the joy of full salvation! Glory, glory, to His name!"

Wow! To freely give everything to Him while trusting Him and living every day in His presence with a burning love for Him. This almost sounds like the only way to achieve a devout, all for Him, lifestyle is to cloister yourself from everything and everyone while existing in total silence and only indulging in those things of necessity that sustain life on earth. You might be thinking here; "I love you God, but I am confused. I have a life and I **am** trying. God, you did give me the desire and ability to live out this life, didn't you?"

Jesus said in Luke 14:33; "Any of you who does not give up everything he has cannot be My disciple." Following much contemplative styled prayer where I asked Jesus to help me know what these words were to mean to me, my interpretation of this verse shifted drastically. For years, I read this as meaning to literally give up all my possessions, all my dreams, all that I had worked for— remember my "I" laden quote in the first sentence of Chapter One. Now what this verse means to me is that for me to be a disciple of Christ I must give up my fears, my arrogance and my ignorance and replace all of that previously wasted space with God's love. But how? By surrendering. Being a "disciple" of Jesus is to live in His image and that to give up everything is to surrender all that encumbers you and keeps you from freely loving, trusting and serving Him.

31

Jesus was human too. He, during His time on Earth, with the exception of sin, experienced all of our struggles, temptations and joys. Jesus, like us, had free will to act as He chose and His choice was to grow in knowledge and understanding and to pursue His faith in God the Father. I want to emphasize part of what I just said; it was His choice to grow in knowledge and understanding and to pursue His faith in God. The operative words here are "to grow." For me, "to grow," or "growth," is synonymous with "knowledge." Jesus grew in His knowledge and understanding of God the Father. Jesus, a devout Jew, was well learned in Jewish Law (the Old Testament for all practical purposes). Jesus also had a supportive resource base in the form of His holy family. Mary and Joseph along with many other God fearing people were instrumental in His growth of religious knowledge.

During Jesus' encounter with Satan in the desert, He chose to see past temptation and focus on what in His heart was the ultimate goal, our salvation. "Then Jesus was led by the Spirit into the desert to be tempted by the devil."

"Jesus said to him, "Get away, Satan! It is written: 'The Lord, your God, shall you worship and him alone shall you serve.'"**6** Jesus grew in knowledge while surrendering all that encumbered Him from freely loving, trusting and serving God.

Christ is, as St. Paul wrote in Colossians; "the image of the invisible God." **7** Our "invisible" yet all knowing and all loving God gave His only Son, Jesus, to die for our sins. He also gave each of us the free will to choose to either live a blessed and purpose filled life for the sake of honoring Him and achieving His promise of eternal life ("God gave us eternal life, and this life is in his Son."**8**) or to never die of self and live this life of decay to its fullest ("Do not store up for yourselves treasures on earth, where moth and decay destroy…"**9**).

In His last three years here on earth, Jesus was so dialed in and so committed to His love for God that He truly knew what surrenderment was all about. He knew His purpose. Jesus saying;…"give up everything…to be My disciple" was Him knowing what was still to come ("Because he surrendered himself to death and was counted among the wicked; And he shall take away the sins of many, and win pardon for their offenses."**10**). Jesus, God incarnate, God in the flesh, wants us to live and enjoy life here on earth but to do so with an unbridled love and respect for God and all of His creation. Jesus wants us to be successful in following Him into eternal life.

The Bible is the Word and therefore the Truth of God's Word is available to those who seek the Truth. If you live in the free world, it is as simple as remembering where you last put or packed your Bible. God forbid the latter might be the case for you. If so, don't fret, I too have had my Bible tucked away for "safe keeping" a time or two. There are those in some countries; however, who would, and who have, die(d) for the opportunity to read the Word.

For many of us it is not oppression or the fear of execution that keeps us from reading the Bible. It is not the mislabeled box from the last move. It is the fear of having to choose whether or not to act on the information that comes from the source of the Truth, the Word. Recall in the previously listed definitions of the word "knowledge" that most contained the word "application" or the word "experience." Though the definitions of "knowledge" vary some, they do, with the exception of Bloom's, all suggest that knowledge is achieved only after the information/data collected and reviewed is experienced or applied in some manner by the one seeking the knowledge.

This may be a good time to shift gears some and move from "knowledge," what is it and where is it, to some reflection on getting to "know" God. It is here that we will also address various practical methods of sourcing "knowledge."

Knowing God is not to know about Him in the abstract or with a guarded disposition. To know God is to enter into His saving grace.

Have you ever thought you really knew a person and later found that you really didn't? Maybe it was that "weird" Uncle or that "better than" co-worker who; because of your predisposition and limited knowledge of them, would always be kept at a comfortable distance if you had any say in the matter. Do you remember how glad you were when you looked up one day and that person you thought you really knew was now your new friend.

To know God is not to struggle philosophically with His eternal essence, but rather to recognize and accept His Truth and to be productive with His gifts and generous with the fruits that accompany His gifts. God is also our Friend and to know Him is to love Him.

Earlier in this chapter we covered that the New Testament of the Bible emphasizes that knowing God is also a response of faith and an acceptance of Christ. It is Christ who made God known as is written early in the book of John; "…the law was given through Moses, grace and truth came through Jesus Christ. No one has ever seen God. The only Son, God, who is at the Father's side, has revealed Him." **11** So, to know Christ is to know God. Toward the end of the book of John it is written; "Now this is eternal life, that they should know You, the only true God, and the one whom You sent, Jesus Christ."**12**

Christ, the Word made flesh, was also talking to you and me when He spoke and revealed so much to the disciples in the days and the hours leading up to His passion and crucifixion. If we can truly listen to the words Jesus speaks in the Gospels as words being spoken directly to us, we will begin to truly know Jesus as Lord and Messiah. If we will surrender our fear, arrogance and ignorance while saying "yes" to the Truth that He is and therefore the Truth He speaks, our hearts will be filled with much joy and our attitude toward and aptitude of religious knowledge will sore to high Heaven.

Up to now we have focused mainly on sourcing religious knowledge and getting to know God through Jesus via the Holy Bible. No doubt, the content of the Holy Bible is the Word and it is through the Word that we gain knowledge and it is through the Word that we hear Jesus and really get to know Him. However, we are blessed with numerous other avenues by which we can source knowledge of the Word and tangibly experience the Word made flesh. I am sure you are already listing several in your mind. Study guides written to coincide with the Bible of your liking. Books and sermons written and delivered by Priest, Pastors and Ministers of Christian based religions. Songs and poems that creatively stimulate our cognitive senses as they speak of His power, grace and love.

All of these are variations of the Word. Actually, the persons behind the resources themselves are great examples of working knowledge. These faithful stewards (disciples / God fearing Christians) chose to collect religious information and found meaningful ways to experience and apply it for the betterment of self and others alike. Beyond that, these same people are actually the eyes, hands and voice of Christ. It is our choice as to whether we listen or not. It was Job who said to his friends while in the desert; "For God does speak, perhaps once, or even twice, though one perceive it not."[13]

When we are directly or indirectly in the presents of those who "love God with all of their hearts, soul and minds…and love their neighbor as they love themselves," we too are in the presence of Christ and it is during these blessed encounters that we can truly get to know God while obtaining additional practical religious knowledge in the process.

As we will address in the next chapter, surrenderment also requires a strengthened and advanced *understanding* of vital and diverse religious knowledge. What can be confusing, at least it is for me, is which one is first, knowledge or understanding. Depending on what verse or from which book you are absorbing the Word; on one hand, the two could easily be viewed as having virtually the same meaning. On the other hand, the two could be perceived as having slightly separate meanings and an obvious order of succession though still being interconnected in some respects.

Despite human logic's baffling quandary of "the chicken or the egg" here, we must not forget that God is Almighty, Wisdom itself. He has a plan and He knows what He is doing. We read in Exodus where the Lord spoke to Moses, saying; "I have filled him *(Bezalel—regarding construction of the sanctuary)* with the Spirit of God in wisdom, in understanding, in knowledge, and in all kinds of craftsmanship...." *(Added notation mine)* **14**

If we are truly open to His Word, He will direct our subjective nature and we will know and or understand Him as our loving Creator who rejoices as we labor to allow Him to bless us with the ability and, yes, the wisdom to serve others through Him.

When I begin to feel overwhelmed in matters such as these and in ones I sometimes get caught up in like the age old stumper of; "should I first put on both socks or one sock / one shoe (same foot) and then repeat," I pause for a moment and calmly pray something along these lines—"God, I'm doing it again. Please give me the wisdom needed to surrender what is weighting me down here and free my mind so that I can discern, choose and move on." I sometimes just say "Jesus, with Your wisdom I will; 'lead with the right foot, relax and let grace happen'." **15**

One of my friend's Mother always says; "lead with the right foot...." By saying "lead with the right foot" what is meant is that we must choose to step out in faith with what we know in our heart is the correct action and direction. This requires us to have readied ourselves by absorbing and living God's word through knowledge and understanding despite their exact order and exact meaning. God's wisdom, if called upon often, will set the course for their individual and collective use and we will continue to be all the more capable to do His bidding. So, for the remained of this book; "relax and let grace happen."

Chapter Three
UNDERSTANDING

Scripture often uses the words knowledge, understanding and wisdom interchangeably. Occasionally, they are isolated and used to convey a specific point. It is here when we should have a developed grasp of the meaning of the individual word in use.

In the previous chapter, we covered, in detail, the topic of "knowledge" as it relates to religious knowledge and its importance relative to really being able to fully surrender to God. To "understand" God's Word we must advance beyond the important act of making time to read the Bible. The same goes for "wisdom." Below is a diagram which differentiates the three terms.

Knowledge	**Understanding**	**Wisdom**
Facts	Meaning	What to Do
Information	Principles	Application
Memory	Reason	Action
Scholars	*Teachers*	*Prophets*1

If knowledge is *facts*, then understanding is the process and ability to lift *meaning* out of the facts obtained and wisdom is knowing *what to do next*. Please do take a moment and follow the similar thought process, from left to right, on the remaining two synonyms to the word "knowledge"; "*information*" and "*memory*."

Note: The last row of the above diagram exists so to draw a biblical connection to the respective columns.

In 1 Corinthians it reads; "To one is given through the Spirit the expression of wisdom; to another the expression of knowledge...." "Some people God has designated in the church to be...teachers...."**2** My interpretation of this scripture when Paul is speaking to the people of Corinth, is that he, at that very moment in time, was addressing a certain grouping of disciples who were being challenged to take full advantage of their specific spiritual gift and to discern what Jesus, the Word made flesh, had empowered them to achieve. Also, I gather that Paul was instructing these disciples to continually and simultaneously combine and share the fruit from their respective gifts with those of varying gifts. Then, with a collective intent, educate, instruct and empower their neighbors who were awaiting the Good News.

Though we may not be as fully enlightened in specific gifts of the Spirit as many were in biblical times, we each do have varying degrees of the gifts of the Holy Spirit available to us. It requires, however, that we "step-up" and begin to develop and use them as God intended.

If we believe in the Triune God, then we have knowledge of and an appreciation for the individual Persons; Father, Son and Holy Spirit. Being that Jesus left us the Holy Spirit, beginning at Pentecost; as we live and grow in our faith we can rest assured that what dwelled in Jesus, while on Earth, dwells in us today, and that is the Holy Spirit. This being said, we can also rest assured that these same gifts are available to us because of what is written in the book of Isaiah; "The Spirit of the Lord shall rest upon Him: A spirit of wisdom and of understanding, a spirit of counsel and of strength, a spirit of knowledge and of fear of the Lord."

Again, we are each created with varying degrees of knowledge, understanding and wisdom and it is incumbent of us to harness these gifts and apply them individually and collectively whenever and where ever the Holy Spirit guides us to do so.

Hopefully me having provided special meaning to the words/gifts of knowledge, understanding and wisdom, has given you a clear vision of the real differences in their functions, as well as an appreciation for their interconnectedness. The gift we will focus on for the remainder of this chapter is that of "understanding." We will cover how to understand religious knowledge derived from various sources of the Word, namely the Bible.

To understand is to be able to abstract the meaning out of information itself. Understanding is to see through the facts and to clearly decipher the relevant dynamics of what, how and why. Understanding is like a microscope designed to enrich the details of the image under glass. However, it is the discretion of the user as to what is taken to full focus and what is left in a blur.

The depth of our understanding is only limited by the measure of our willingness to conceptualize and put to work well founded knowledge. Let me repeat this; *the depth of our understanding is only limited by the measure of our willingness to conceptualize and put to work well founded knowledge*. To truly understand is to extrude founding principles from information that we can further apply as we yearn to know, love and serve God all the more.

Okay. So let's say that you are sitting in your favorite chair reading an article from the church bulletin that is about a specific scripture quote. Or maybe you are in a weekly bible study group and your bible (you finally found it—good for you) is open to a specific book. In either case let's assume for a second here that the facts, the information, is soaking into your memory. Now let's say that just before you choose to put away the Bulletin or just before someone in your study group discovers cookies on the back table, you have, for a fleeting moment, an impulse that causes you to say, or think: "Hmmm." That "Hmmm" is your God given gift of understanding stepping up and wanting to be used. At that very moment you have generated a mental "red flag" that wants badly to remind you or to encourage you to abstract meaning out of knowledge; to make reason out of what your logical mind has absorbed or taken to memory. You just fed your mind and it wants to process the data or facts. That cookie may have to wait its turn.

My point. When we are in the mindset to understand as we continue to surrender (so to live in and perpetuate the Divine love of God), we must learn to recognize this "whisper" and give it due attention in a reasonable manner. I intentionally said, "reasonable." We still have a life to live; kids that need to be bathed, bills to be paid, cookies to be eaten.

When you become aware that your mind is saying "Hmmm" relative to religious knowledge that has come your way, you must be prepared to somehow "earmark" the data for future reference and for further review. You must have a reliable method in place otherwise you are going to loose the drive and focus needed to come back to it and you will give justification of the diversion to the pressures or the pleasures of the here and now.

Many people choose to journal. They have it set in their mind that following the reading of select material, and some quiet time for reflection (some call this contemplative prayer) they will then pose to themselves various questions and log their response accordingly. Examples of some questions might be; "What did that really mean to me?"; "How does this apply to my life as a Christian?"; "What

41

guiding principles or what rule of thumb should I or will I apply to this knowledge?."

Over the course of the past three years while going through some rather trying times; which I will appropriately share throughout this book, I adopted or maybe I should say adapted a method I have used for over twenty five years in business. Due to the nature of the work I performed, the number of jobs or projects underfoot at one time were many and the volume of variables within each project were also at high count. Though many areas of variability within several of the projects had a similar ring to them, it is still fair to say the task to manage them all together was at times daunting. I am sure you get the picture and most likely you are there at this moment or you have been there in the past regardless your vocation in life.

The method I used was to collect the information pertaining to the situation at hand and deduce it into a mental story. Then, when time permitted; at night in the hotel or on the plane to the next and most pressing project, I would recap the situation or event in narrative form (2-3 paragraphs with bullets where suitable). It is important to note here that either due to sleep deprivation, cultural aggravation, ignorance and or arrogance, often I would be just a little "peeved" over how something went or how I was loosing control of a situation and while writing, my narrative recap would turn into a narrative rant. Nonetheless, I would capture the data as clearly and objectively as possible at the time and then "let it soak" for a while.

Sometimes I waited just one hour, but most of the time I didn't come back to the recap for at least 8-10 hours. I would then highlight the factual data, chuckle at some of the rants and begin to evaluate/ assess and process the data in a manner that allowed me to see the flow or the system within. I would apply Management Technology styled tools of "system thinking" and "problem solving" to ascertain what was behind the apparent problem or opportunity. "What were its drivers and why?" Why was it responding or being responded to in the manner it was?" A tool I always used was that of asking why five times to get to the root cause.3

When I felt I "understood" the situation and was well equipped, not only with facts but also with the means to proceed with action suited to resolve the problem or maximize the opportunity, I would present my finding and my understanding to parties of interest and or those with shared responsibilities and would begin to work with them in tandem to achieve a perceived goal.

I would always keep my narrative recaps in their raw form and put them in a file labeled "scrub notes." I can't really tell you why I called them "scrub notes," maybe it was all of those Hospital Soap Operas I watched in College just before class or in place of class. Regardless, I kept them to come back to for help on similar events in the future. If nothing else, I would have them as a guide and to restore my confidence when I doubted myself and any past successes I thought I might have once had.

I now mirror this method, at least in theory, during those times when I am applying my God given gifts of knowledge, understanding and, yes even, wisdom toward my responsibility and privilege to live in and to perpetuate the Divine love of God. Below are the steps I try to adhere to:

Approach the Bible like you would a good novel or the Christmas letter from a dear friend.

Experience the Bible. Try to visualize the event you are reading as if you are right there.

Place yourself in the mindset of the person speaking and or being spoken to or about. You may have to read a passage several times or come back to it later.

Set time aside to reflect some, contemplatively. Ask God to speak to your heart and to send the message meant for you right at that moment even though the passage was written many, many years ago.

Recap the facts and try to extract true meaning for you to apply in your life.

Gather often with some prayer partners or "Bible buddies" that share your interest in the Truth and try to formulate decisive action best suited to help correct or improve situations or relationships in your life while positively impacting their lives and the lives of others.

Establish a trusting relationship with a spiritual advisor and allow him or her to counsel you based on their qualified and inspired knowledge and understanding of the Word.

Don't be satisfied with simply reading the Bible. Commit to studying it too. A casual understanding of the Bible may not be enough to receive God's message to you. The Bible says many things, and if not careful, you can misconstrue the true meaning if you do not come to a thorough understanding of its teachings. Study the scriptures for meaning and guiding principles.

Be open to the helping hand of other people who share your passion. Make sure the person or persons you have help you are well grounded in their faith and love for God. Be selective but not judgmental. You are looking to broaden the understanding of what God has to say in the Word and not just the opinion of someone else. An opinion with no substance is like a tree with no roots, simply just another stick in the mud—no fruit here.

Ask those you partner with to pray for you and, of course, you do the same in kind. Their wisdom may save you from a poor decision in your life. It is written in the book of James; "If any of you lacks wisdom, he should ask God, who gives generously to all without finding fault, and it will be given to him."**4** Most often when we pray for wisdom, God calls us into fellowship with believers who can provide an answer.

Be careful to not allow your impressions or false impressions to shadow the facts. It is likely life is going to throw you a curve ball about the time knowledge, facts of the Bible, is beginning to have meaning. You may get the impression that what you thought was factual no longer is, due to the mess you have to deal with despite your perceived "understanding." This is where the prayer for wisdom really helps. It is reassuring to have the objective Word of God confirmed, validated, especially in the times of doubt.

Rest assured, God will lead us as we give of ourselves (surrender) to the understanding of His word and the guidance of the Holy Spirit. He will enable us to become good decision makers; people who base actions on moral principles and the spiritual wisdom found in the Bible. The Holy Spirit will guide us to and through the Truth which is the Word of God.

As we come to the close of Part I, Surrenderment, it is important to point out that much is expected of us if we choose to truly surrender to God. Likewise, much is available to us as we quest to achieve our eternal end, salvation in Heaven. Recall the central theme of this book; Surrenderment is a continuous process. It requires an enduring faith, a mature sense of purpose and the determined will to forgo the lures and direct assault from evil in our midst as we quest for eternal life with God the Father.

The requirements mentioned in the theme; faith, purpose and a strong will make up the remaining three parts of this book. My intention here was to isolate these rather broad areas of expectation and break each down into bite size pieces so that by the end of the book we will have come full circle and will possess a strengthened awareness for what it takes to fully surrender to God.

To pray that God's will be done requires much belief. Through knowledge and understanding of the Word, our belief is fortified and belief in what is to come is a sign of faith. For us to steady the course and not loose ground along the way, we must endure many trails while under the cross; hence the heading of Part II—Enduring Faith.

PART II
ENDURING FAITH

Chapter Four
PERCEIVED FAILURE

"Do not throw away your confidence, which has a great reward. For you have need of endurance, so that you may do the will of God and receive what is promised...Now faith is the assurance of things hoped for, the conviction of things not seen." **1**

The first part of the above scripture quote from the book of Hebrews; "Do not throw away your confidence," sounds like a challenge to me. The author seems to be on his toes and anticipates a tired and distraught "why?" to be asked or contemplated by the recipient, so he continues with; "...which has great reward."

I love a good challenge. I also love to ask questions. Being that scripture is written for all who believe or want to believe and that each person is being talked to directly through the writings, it is no wonder the author of Hebrews prepared this text as he did. So as I read on, my next mental question is; what *is this "great reward" that comes to those who do not "throw away" confidence?* The author's reply is; "endurance." *Why do I need endurance?* "So that you may do the will of God."

Not to over simplify things here but let's bring into the picture Part I of this book, namely chapters two and three; Knowledge and Understanding. Okay, we have collected knowledge or information from the Word in Hebrews. We have read it and attempted to absorb its content. Further, meaning has been extracted from the content of the Word read and we have clearly deciphered the relevant dynamic of "why?" We seem to understand what the author is getting at and what God is saying to us in the here and now. But hold on a minute; if we move forward in faith, if we proceed in faith, what happens if and when we experience failure along the way? What then? The author must have been ready for this question too. "Faith is the assurance of things hoped for, the conviction of things not seen."

See, enduring faithfully is working through the pain despite the present discomfort and doing so with the conviction that what we hope for will soon be actualized. Even amidst the shadow of failure, whether cast by the perception of someone else or from that of our own making, we must humble ourselves and patiently preserver in faith. Because as the author of Hebrews wrote further on in the same chapter; "without faith, it is impossible to please God." **2**

This chapter; "Perceived Failure," leads off Part II; Enduring Faith." Why?, you ask. I was ready for that question. Because if we are going to truly surrender to God, we must keep our minds and our hearts full of knowledge and understanding of God's will and we must push on in faith, in belief, even when we fail or experience what is perceived as failure. We must rise to the occasion and take on the challenge to "not throw away our confidence," and we must take true inventory of our not so pleasant experiences in life and acknowledge the value or future value from both the scare and the scar. Whether you thought you failed in a particular circumstance or you have what you consider as proof of failure—the documented results of a dismal midterm exam or the dully counted and certified audit of returns from a school board run off election gone south—this near miss or direct hit, is chucked full of vital experiences that will do nothing but bolster your future and furthered success so long as you endure in faith.

If we remain downtrodden about what we perceive as failure and never "take courage" **3** and try again, we may never learn how much we have grown as a result of our experiences; our perceived failures. We must have faith in God. I once heard a man say; "faith proves our endurance and our endurance proves our faith." **4**

Early in my professional career, I was eager to impress my peers and the "higher-ups" in the company I represented. Being I was in the field more so than the cubical and my trips to the "corporate office" were few and far between, when I had my chance I would try so hard to prove my worth and advance my career for the eyes of others. During one meeting at the corporate offices, in what was a session on corporate culture, the group I was in was asked to recap its thoughts relative to the material discussed throughout the week long meeting. I recall having been so enthralled in the subject matter and stimulated by the group interaction. When selecting a spokesperson for our group, I was thrusting my arm in the air with similar enthusiasm as that of Horshack on the hit sitcom in the 1970's, "Welcome Back Cotter." Before I knew it, I was at the podium in front of no less than one hundred of my peers and some very influential executives.

What happened next had the shattering emotional impact equal to that of a fifty pound sledge hammer slamming into a china cabinet. I stepped up, eager to address my peers, not only about the topic of corporate culture; which I was very interested in, but also for the reason of making my mark and proving to all present that I too was a professional.

You know the drill, my tongue became dry and the muscles in my neck cramped like a runner's calves screaming for potassium. No one in the audience appeared to be naked; believe me I quickly tried to envision them as such. I was the one who felt naked. Naked of the ability to formulate a rational thought much less draw a full breath. Naked of the self confidence, the upbeat attitude and strong aptitude I just had seconds before I "thumped the microphone." I was told later that my painful inability to proceed ended with me apologizing and asking an "up and coming" peer and friend from within my group to step up and speak in my place.

The remaining hour of the meeting was a blur. The three hour flight back to the field was lonely. The next month or so consisted of me replaying my five minutes to failure over and over in my head. My self esteem was shattered like the china cup after having encountered the hammer. I recall thinking; "my professional career is over" as I contemplated quitting and moving back home."

Earlier I said that not so pleasant experiences in life are chucked full of value and that they can bolster our future success, provided we preserver. We must be courageous and have faith in God and push ourselves to overcome the adverse effects of a perceived failure. If not, this experience could potentially lead to a spiritual disconnect.

As devastating as my experience was at the time and despite the scare it gave me relative to ever again wanting to speak in front of my peers and the scar of having not achieved my intended objective, I did preserver. Through my enduring faith in God, I turned to Him and prayed for the strength to overcome what felt like a tremendous personal and professional failure. As He always does, God answered my prayer.

I relied on my Dad and we spoke often in the evenings on the phone (me in Chicago and Dad in Corpus Christi). Dad reminded me of other self perceived failures in my life. My all out efforts to be "first string" lineman on the football team during High School while only occasionally obtaining this level of achievement a couple of times during my senior year. My having left the scene of an auto accident, during my first year in College, after the prompting of the other party I had collided with. Me booking over ninety credit hours at a Junior

College and only being able to transfer some sixty hours toward my goal to earn a bachelor degree at the University I was about to attend, if I could muster the grades.

Again, Dad was reminding me of what I had once viewed as failures and how bleak my outlook on future success was at the time that each occurred. In retrospect, each provided me with a chink or two of armor that I could add to my overall suit of armor worn while persevering through life's battles. Having these so called failures brought to my attention and being able to look back and recognize that each resulted in success, had a profound effect on how I perceived and managed failure into the future.

Other mentors and caring people, like that of my Dad, prayed with me and counseled me to move on in my pursuit to grow as a business professional and to set a plan of action to achieve reaffirming successes that form a critical path toward renewal and improvement more so than approval and vindication.

This advice, coupled with me taking the courage to engage, brought me out of a down spiral of self doubt. Within a rather short period of time I was back to my confident self, openly and enthusiastically communicating to others while being less concerned over whether or not I was at par with or accepted by my peers.

The main action I took; which I do to this day, is to be fully prepared before I speak publicly and to harness my emotion during the process. I strived to control my emotion and not allow my emotion to control me. Additionally, I started small and joined a local chapter of Toastmasters International and began to attend monthly meetings. This allowed me to experience renewed success while speaking publicly in somewhat of a controlled environment. Over time, I began to speak at various venues, starting small and then adding on as I felt the calling and the confidence.

This once perceived failure, of several in my life, and the faithful action to preserver with confidence has and will continue to be a positive value add event for me and has resulted in much satisfaction and success. I know that God is pleased that I and others are willing to look at what is lacking in our lives and to step up in faith and to make great strides toward pleasing Him and not giving up or loosing faith due to the perception of failure.

The experience I shared with you could easily be viewed as a "walk in the park" if stacked up against the hardships of others throughout the world. Recall me mentioning in the "Forward" the young girl born to the addicted mother and the forty year old man loosing his leg due to diabetes. The severity of suffering that people experience varies greatly, yet when an experience in life is viewed as a failure I am convinced the feeling of disparity is one that every person can say they know intimately and have had to carry, if not for just a moment or two. For each of us, the thought of failure draws up an unsavory emotion; one none of us want to experience nor endure for any period of time.

To say Christ failed or perceived Himself as having failed throughout His life might upset a host of Theologians, but it is my opinion that Jesus, as a human being on Earth, did experience the perception of failure. Though He did not resort to any sinful act nor did He do anything less than His Father's will, He had to have felt discouraged or distraught at times. I wish to sight the following scripture to support my opinion.

1) News of John the Baptist's beheading—"His (John's) disciples came and took away the corpse and buried him; and they went and told Jesus. When Jesus heard of it, he withdrew in a boat to a deserted place by himself."**5**

2) Jesus while on the Cross—"My God, my God, why have you forsaken me?"**6**

My point. Even Christ had His doubts and times of discouragement; those times where He questioned whether His efforts were going to result as envisioned. If everyone we know, especially Christ, has at one time or another experienced "perceived failure," then we can at least take solace in this and build from there when we too encounter what is initially viewed as a stand alone failure or as a weight placed on us that is unfair and unbearable.

Two things St. Paul said comes to mind in this regard; "Because He Himself was tested through what He suffered, He is able to help those who are being tested."7 "God is faithful and will not let you be tried beyond your strength; but with the trial He will also provide a way out, so that you may be able to bear it."8

Look, even a piece of string has the making of a long and durable rope. Your setback(s) can still result in success. It takes you having "the conviction of things not seen"—faith (believing the string can someday be a rope). It requires you persevering and continually taking positive and reassuring steps (collecting the individual pieces of string you find). It takes you building momentum while fortifying and renewing your ability to succeed (weaving the pieces of string together to achieve a rope of desired length and strength).

If you are thinking; "Why do I need to endure?," recall what is written in Hebrews; "so that you may do the will of God."

In the opening of Chapter One, I shared what I once feared about "surrendering" based on my level of knowledge and even faith at the time. Recall me saying; "If I surrender, I will have given up all that I have worked for, all that I have anguished over, all that I have dreamed to achieve." This statement is very similar to what we think when we have failed. "Oh, no! Now I am a failure, I have lost all that I have worked for, all of the success I had dreamed to achieve."

If we retool our way of thinking when it comes to failure and begin to see the value or future value in what we just experienced, we will then be that much more willing and able to surrender to God and partake in His plan. Allow me to make an attempt at crafting a leading statement to recite soon after experiencing the unsavory emotions of a perceived failure or a setback of sorts.

"Lord, that was not what I expected, but it is what happened and I will rebound. I will take inventory of what I learned and adapt my actions accordingly. I will faithfully proceed and, with Your hand, succeed in and for Your glory."

"By Humility, and the fear of the Lord, are riches, honor and life." Proverbs 22:4

Chapter Five
HUMILITY

I am sure we have all heard the song by Mac Davis that has the repeating verse of; "Oh Lord it's hard to be humble when you're perfect in every way." Though meant as tongue and cheek, this line is something that you have probably felt on occasions. I know I have. I might not have ever really said it directly to God but through my actions I demonstrated it, nonetheless. If we were to agree that humility is the lack of false pride, then thinking we are "perfect in every way" would be loaded with false pride. None of us are perfect. We all sin and without God's grace and mercy, we have no means to even exist on our own merit. I don't know about you but I have those times when I am so full of myself (I just did a kind act or maybe someone told me how good of a man I was) and before I know it, I enter a situation where someone either serves me below my expectation or says something that attempts to deflate my ego and I respond or retaliate with action and or words that are pride filled, plus a little. I immediately assume the other person is inferior to me and attack his or her actions or words with no regard to whether they may be right or that they may just not be having a very good day.

The opposite of humility is pride. Being prideful is the act of arrogating **1** one's self to the attributes that God created him or her with in the first place. Remember Genesis 1:27; "God created man in His image." Pride is by no means a reflective image of God.

Maybe a revised verse to Mr. Davis' song that we should hum along to is; "Oh Lord it's hard to be humble, like You who is perfect in every way." This line would at least support the premise that humility is the trait of recognizing and acknowledging things as they really are. God is perfect in every way and it is extremely difficult to be humble, to be absent of self pride as we make our way through life here on Earth.

In Chapter 4 I talked about perceived failures and how a specific act or event may at the time not appear to be a success or have any value toward future successes. I said that if we preserver and "retool our way of thinking…and begin to see the value…in what we just experienced, we will then be that much more willing and able to surrender to God and partake in His plan."

Part of the process to "retool our way of thinking" so that we can be successful at surrenderment; so that we can endure in faith, is to humble ourselves in both thoughts and actions. The Easton Bible dictionary defines humility as a state of mind well pleasing to God. Further, Easton supports its definition with the following scriptural quote from 1 Peter 3:3-4; "Your adornment should not be an external one,…but rather the hidden character of the heart, expressed in the imperishable beauty of a gentle and calm disposition, which is precious in the sight of God."

Though in this passage the author was speaking of the expected conduct of a wife toward her husband, the message was still being addressed to all Christian followers in a hostile world at the time. **2** "A gentle and calm disposition, which is precious in the sight of God."

This part of the above verse reminds me of Jesus' Sermon on the Mount where He begins to teach the Beatitudes, namely; "Blessed are the meek," "Blessed are they who hunger and thirst for righteousness," Blessed are the merciful," Blessed are the pure in heart," Blessed are the peacemakers." **3**

The choice to be humble must be attached to our innate quality where we are drawn to be courteous to and respectful of others. Humility is the opposite of aggressiveness, arrogance, boastfulness and vanity. Humility is the quality that allows us to go out of our way to meet and serve the needs and demands of others while putting our own needs and demands on hold or at least in second seat for the time being.

The lack of humility ushers in angry words and actions that, regardless how small or incidental at the time, can result in dissolved relationships such as marriages and long standing friendships. Despite the means of delivery, our pride can do a world of hurt to those we once loved or those we want to love and who need our love in this world.

We must strive to have a humbled heart if we plan to endure in faith. How else are we to maintain a faithful exuberance if we are walking down a path paved with self absorbed motives. Recall the quote from Hebrews; "Do not throw away your confidence." This is speaking of confidence in God (faithfulness) not confidence in our self guided, therefore selfish, actions. How can we expect to not throw away our confidence in God if all we do is long for and pursue what appears as sustained pleasure or at least immediate satisfaction.

A very well know scripture passage is that of Matthew 7:13-14 where Jesus said; "Enter through the narrow gate; for the gate is wide and the way is broad that leads to destruction, and there are many who enter through it. For the gate is small and the way is narrow that leads to life, and there are few who find it." I visualize the path least traveled (road to salvation) as being on a rather steep uphill grade in very rough and rocky terrain. The underbrush blocks the view of what is truly underfoot and with the exception of an occasional glimpse of bare rock (rock bottom) you are left to forge your way ahead with only hope as your companion while you hope that you are on the right course. You don't know exactly what to expect and you fear that you may miss it in the blink of an eye.

When we are doing as Jesus taught in the Beatitudes, we are acting in faith and if we truly believe, then we "are blessed" and we will: "inherit the earth," be filled," "obtain mercy," "see God" and be "called children of God." **4** The same is true for those who follow us; those who turn to God because of our humility. Just think, because of your selfless, merciful act(s), another person who was on the way to destruction and headed for the wide gate turned to follow you. Imagine this person changing course and choosing to follow your lead, yes, along that narrow way toward salvation. I am sure you would be extremely excited, but wouldn't you be equally as concerned that this person following you in faith might fall off course? Sure you would.

What would kick in is more of your selfless nature. You would adorn the hidden character of your heart, "expressed in the imperishable beauty of a gentle and calm disposition." Your own needs and demands would have taken back seat to those of your neighbor and that; "is precious in the sight of God." At that point, your faith in God would have been validated and you would strive even harder to clear the way to eternity for not only yourself but for the many that were now in tow. Just before speaking of the narrow and wide gates, Jesus spoke these words; "In everything, therefore, treat people the same way you want them to treat you." Matt. 7:12.

I have read that humility is "the avenue to glory." **5** The term avenue generally brings up the image of a well marked and lighted thoroughfare leading to the most sought out destinations in the area that caters to our individual needs. However, in terms of salvation, for His glory, we must humble ourselves and joyfully prepare for the assent along the narrow way home. We will fall. We may even get passed by; but if we are focused on the "eternal end" and selflessly are working to serve others with a "gentle and calm disposition," then even the one doing the passing will stop and render aid. Jesus was speaking to all people when He said "treat people the same way you want them to treat you."

God often uses intense pressure and adversity to humble us and refocus our thoughts so that we begin to think the way He thinks. I have heard it said there are four "safety checks" that God will use "to keep us from being prideful and arrogant" (the opposite of being humble). The four safety checks are; 1) pain, 2) embarrassment, 3) criticism and 4) hardship. **6**

When I first heard of these safety checks, I was quite cynical. I thought, "safety my hat. What is safe about being in pain or encountering hardship?" I then recalled the many trials that people such as King David and Job were put through and how they each recognized and accepted God's hand in their suffering. Though each anguished, if not flat out griped at times, they continued to submit with a humbled heart and responded in alignment with God's will. King David said in Psalms 109:25; "I have become a mockery to them; when they see me, they shake their heads." Job said in Job 9:16-17; "If I appealed to Him and He answered my call,...with a tempest He might overwhelm me, and multiply my wounds without cause."

It is interesting to note that with both King David and Job, God had made favorable mention of both before each began to experience their intense pressure and adversity. David was only ten years old when the prophet Samuel announced to Saul, King of Israel, that David was "a man after His (God's) own heart." **7** Job was living a very blessed life when God spoke to Satan saying; "there is no one like him, blameless and upright, fearing God and avoiding evil." **8**

I make note of this because these men were sinners just like you and me and God knows everything even before it happens. My point. When we are a little down and our self-esteem needs a boost, we should take solace in the fact that God thought/thinks so highly of each of us that He gave Jesus and Jesus gave His life for our sins. We are all special in the eyes of God and He has great plans for each of us.

In chapter 15 of the book of John, Jesus speaks to the Apostles in the vineyard. He goes to great lengths to impress on them the vital importance of us being pruned so to bear much fruit. Jesus' discourse begins with; "I am the true vine, and my Father is the vine grower. He takes away every branch in me that does not bear fruit, and everyone that does he prunes so that it bears more fruit."**9**

Bruce Wilkerson, author of Prayer of Jabez, wrote another book; Secrets of the Vine, which was entirely devoted to John Chapter 15. I strongly recommend you read Bruce's book; Secrets of the Vine. To those of you who have already read it, I am confident you have a much stronger appreciation for why we experience set backs or perceived failures even when we think we are on course and are advancing at a strong pace.

By human nature, we naturally response to what is not pleasing to our senses by either hesitating or acting to dispel or negate what is perceived as an obtrusion. That is not always a bad thing. If you are out for an evening stroll and you cross path with a rattlesnake or a primed and ready skunk, you might want to take heed to your senses and quickly do a risk/reward assessment just before you faint.

As Christians, we will continue to be faced with trials or setbacks and just like the encounter with the snake, we have a choice in how we can proceed. We can choose to feel defeated and turn away with a bitter resolve to never take a stroll in life again or we can humble ourselves and submit to God's fortifying grace and allow Him to guide us and our neighbors to our just reward.

On a recent stroll through life where my wife, Crickett, and I encountered both the snake and the skunk, I can assure you God had His check list out and ready. The stroll I am referring to was circumstances leading up to us choosing to give professional closure to an industrial services company we founded and successfully operated for thirteen years. I will spare you the details but we received a good dose of pains, embarrassments, criticisms and related hardships for several years following our decision. What I wish to emphasize is not the successful thirteen year run of our business nor the years of trials following its closure; what I wish to emphasize is the choice we made.

Crickett and I didn't want to close our company. However, we knew what was driving the discomforts we were beginning to experience and we had a pretty good handle on risk/reward for those vital few scenarios we had to select from, so we chose. What we first chose was to sideline our options for about two weeks and we prayed for strength and guidance. Mind you, we had been praying together for many years but our, or at least my, prayers always seemed to be a little more conditional when it came to the sustainability of our company. My conditional prayers usually had strategically placed words in them such as "if," "but" and "provided."

This time, as stressed and invested as we were, we collectively chose to go into what I like to call "contemplative lockdown." We separated ourselves from the emotional aspects of the situation at hand while openly and reverently asking

God to guide our hearts. Of course during those days of prayerful deliberation we were still subject to all the variables of day to day living. We kept our focus and committed ourselves to surrendering all that we had and all that we aspired to be and allowed God to guide us through not only a good decision but also the unconditional acceptance of the future events resulting from the decision made.

Humility will help change the way we view God. It will help temper our selfish drive to control that which we have no control over. With humility, we can learn to submit our heart to God (surrender) and allow Him to be in the forefront of our lives. Embracing humility does not mean you have low self-esteem. On the contrary, it develops a sense of lasting courage that is based in and backed by the accepted fact that strength and wisdom needed to do His will is available in, with and through Jesus Christ.

I close this chapter with a passage from the Bible found in 1 Peter 5:5-7; "Clothe yourselves with humility in your dealings with one another, for; "God opposes the proud but bestows favor on the humble. So humble yourselves under the mighty hand of God, that He may exalt you in due time. Cast all your worries upon Him because He cares for you."

Chapter Six
PATIENCE

Have you ever been driving and while entering an expressway, the car in the merging outside lane is matching your speed and appears to almost be taunting you? While your blood pressure begins to elevate your heart also tries to remind you that two wrongs do not make a right. However, your human nature immediately presents a compelling argument that a hard left would at least take out the rear quarter panel of the approaching nuisance.

When agitated and simply spent of any slack in our taunt rope of patience, we frequently say, do or think something just as bad or worse than what was done to us. Often, our patience does not give delay to our wrath long enough for our humility to kick in. As covered in the last chapter, humility is extremely important in our quest to endure in faith as we surrender ourselves to God's will. An equally as important virtue, gifted to us all by the Holy Spirit, is that of patience.

Throughout the Old Testament, God showed much patience by tempering His own wrath. God minimized, prolonged and even removed the treat of His wrath in times where those faithful to Him, namely prophets, would plead for God to show mercy to His people. One account was while Moses was meeting with God on Mount Sinai. The Israelites became ancy and convinced Aaron to allow them to worship idols again during Moses' absence. Seeing this, God said to Moses; "I see how stiff-necked this people is…Let me alone, then, that My wrath may blaze up against them to consume them." **1** Moses made a strong case to God, saying; "Why, O LORD, should your wrath blaze up against your own people, whom you brought out of the land of Egypt."**2** Following much discussion, God "relented in the punishment He had threatened to inflict" **3** and Moses "came down the mountain with two tablets of the commandments in his hands." **4**

Here, as throughout the Old Testament, God showed much patience when humbly confronted by those chosen to lead and prophesize. God harnessed His warranted wrath out of love. He saw where some latitude might aid in the reformation of those who were wavering in their new found faith.

Later in the New Testament, we find Jesus showing much patience too. There are so many examples to choose from but the one that stands out to me is at the feeding of the five thousand near Capernaum. Jesus had recently sent the apostles out to witness "two by two." **5**

Upon their return Jesus was eager to hear their astounding stories of success, but He saw a crowd of people gathering "like sheep without a Shepherd" and "His heart was moved with pity for them." **6** He asks them, the apostles, to feed the people who had assembled and they replied; "five loaves and two fish are all we have here." **7** Jesus patiently asks them to have the people sit down and then proceeded with the blessing and multiplication of the loaves and the fishes.

Jesus knew the apostles could do what He ended up doing Himself, but opted to give the apostles a little slack (my interpretation) and not burst their bubble being they had just come back from doing so much good. Jesus was patient long enough to allow His own humility to kick in and turned His attention, His mercy, to those who hungered.

I find it comforting that God and Jesus, pure love/no sin, gave us such great examples of virtues like that of patience. We should always go to God's Word (knowledge), understand it and then apply it to our own lives. God will work through us and empower us to patiently endure as we trust in Him.

Not only are Jesus' many examples of patience and humility of great comfort when we are down and out and feeling we have no more to give; they too should stand as towering reminders of the awesome and unconditional love God has for us. God, perfect and all-powerful, created us in His image and after making several covenants in the time of the Old Testament, God still shows His love and makes yet another covenant and gives us His only Son. Not just His earthly existence and His tireless signs of what being a true disciple entails, God gives us His son Jesus who in turn gives of His blood for **our** sins. "There is no greater love than this to lay down one's live for one's friends." **8**

When we have had about all of the senseless dribble and haughty action from others that we can handle, we can look to the patience of Jesus and remember that He gave every drop of His blood for our sins and He did nothing to deserve this suffering, accept love us unconditionally. It is with this humbling reminder that we too may be able to harness our wrath out of love for our fellowman.

We are called to be patient not only when others are acting against us but also at times when we feel that we have been forgotten by others and when we have little to no apparent momentum in our lives. In these times, you might almost wish you had someone messing with you just to experience some form of interaction.

I shared with you in Chapter 5 about Crickett and me choosing to close our company. Recall me mentioning that we struggled for several years as a result of our decision. Our struggles did have financial ties to them because we had voluntarily closed the company and effectively stopped all revenue to our household.

Though we had some reserves, thanks to God, we did not envision me being unemployed any longer than three to six months after completing the "closure" related responsibilities we had to administer on behalf of our company. Our struggles also had other drivers. We struggled with the fears of the unknown and the deafening silence that comes when you get little to no feedback during an aggressive campaign to find a job.

I know, I know, you are starting to flip back to the pages where I said; "We kept our focus and…allowed God to guide us through…future events resulting from the decision made." It is true that we made this commitment and valiant efforts to stay the course, but we did still struggle with not so humble feelings at times and the near non existence of patience occasionally as well.

Early in the process of closing the company and preparing to re-enter the work force, there was a Sunday just before Labor Day that I will never forget. One of the readings was from the book of Job and "patience" was the collective message between all the readings and the Homily given by the Priest. As we were exiting the Church, a friend who knew some about what we were experiencing, approached me and said; "when I look at you and Crickett, what comes to mind is the patience of Job."

By the time we got home, I had replayed the words "patience of Job" in my head no less than one thousand times. I kept thinking; "Job must have no patience then because I sure the heck don't." After having discussed it over with Crickett we declined an invitation to go to a Labor Day party at a friend's home. I slowly and intently read the Book of Job throughout the remainder of the day. I tried to let every word soak in. I was determined to know Job. If he was a patient man in my opinion, following the reading, then I was going to see if I could possibly try to emulate him as I struggled with the silence and the snubs coming from the job market.

More than a year later, I was still looking for work. Due to the help I had gained from the Book of Job, I had read it many times over, I was able to preserver. I could relate to Job's determination to not let his pain overshadow his love for God while still wishing he could be pulled out of the game being he was tired of not gaining any ground. ("The Lord gave and the Lord has taken away. Blessed be the name of the LORD." Job:1:21 "Let the day perish on which I was to be born." Job 3:3)

One Sunday afternoon while our family was sitting together in the living room, our youngest daughter, Sami, who was eight years old at the time, picked up my Bible from the end table next to where she was sitting and began to flip through it. Sami was turning chapter by chapter using the labeled tabs as a handle. About a minute passed and then Sami, who was looking at the tab labeled for the book of Job, said; "Hey Dad, you should read here to help you find a job."

We all had a great laugh, not at her expense but we found humor in the fact that the word spelled J_O_B only had one meaning to Sami. I guess it was her innocence more than anything that caught our attention. Her sisters poked fun at Sami a little while Crickett and I marveled at how aware and caring Sami was of the situation at hand.

The following morning, Monday, a day I had grown to dread, I sat to read from the Bible as I always did before hitting the bricks or the computer in search for work. My Bible was marked at the end of Psalms Chapter 26 where I had last read. I was reluctant to read much less try again to go find work. Simply put, I was out of patience and I was not real pleased with God in all honesty. My mind shifted to Sami and what she had said the day before. My eyes filled with tears because I remembered how excited she was and how much faith was behind her suggestion.

I went to the Book of Job and started impatiently flipping through it while in my mind saying; "OK God show me something. Help me out here." My eyes immediately locked onto Job 6:11 and they began to fill again with tears as I read along; "What strength have I that I should endure, and what is my limit that I should be patient?" I was now more confused and as mad as ever.

Again, in my mind; "Are you toying with me here. I know what my questions are. What about some answers?" After saying "I'm sorry" between each sob, I finished ripping through the book of Job and began to read Chapter 27 of Psalms.

By then I was calm. Right out of the box I got the first answer to my two part question from Job 6:11. Psalm 27:1 read; "The Lord is my light and my salvation;…of whom am I afraid?" I was sitting straight up at this point. God had my attention. "The second answer to my two part question has got to be next." Verse two; "Nope that's not it." Verse three; "No." As I finally got to the last verse of the chapter; verse 14, there it was; "Wait for the Lord, take courage; be stouthearted, wait for the Lord!"

My next thought was that I should consider interviewing with Kimberly-Clark who produces Kleenex. Maybe they give out sample packs to new hires.

God had sent a message to me through the innocence of a child when my strength and my patience were at an all time low. I was beginning to doubt Him. God let me know that He heard my questions and that He was there with the answers. I joyfully thanked God, marked my Bible at the end of Psalm chapter 27 and proceeded to go search for a J_O_B with renewed strength and patience.

Earlier in this chapter I said; We should always go to God's Word (knowledge), understand it and then apply it to our own lives. God will work through us and empower us to patiently endure as we trust in Him. A Bible verse that supports this is from Romans; "Everything written in the Scriptures was written to teach us, in order that we might have hope through the patience and encouragement which the Scriptures give us."**9**

Whether we are drawn to patience in the time of disparity or when others are lashing out with false accusations; we must remember, in that moment, that we chose (freewill) to take the high and narrow road. No doubt, it is much easier to crumble under pressure than it is to bear the strain of its weight. It is true that striking back requires little effort compared to the immense restraint required when turning the other cheek.

The Apostle James wrote; "consider it all joy, my brethren, when you encounter various trials, knowing that the testing of your faith produces patience."**10** It seems strange to be joyful when we are about to under go discomfort. What makes this advice; "consider it all joy," so appealing to Christians is that we can undergo the trial as a sign of homage and thanks to Christ for Him having endured so much, even death, for us. Also, we can rest assured that we will emerge stronger in faith because the Holy Spirit will bath us in His gifts all the more.

God needs us to have patience and a humbled heart so He can mold us into His perfect image. Score carding or measuring what we experience in life based on our personal wants and likes works against God's efforts to help transform us. We should look at our every experience, our every action, in life as an opportunity to allow God unrestricted access into our hearts. We each greatly benefit from the added capacity to respond in His likeness when we submit in this way, when we submit to "the way."**11**

To faithfully endure suffering, we must take up our Cross and see all experiences in life as being loaded with spiritual value. We must look to the great examples we have in Christ as He so lovingly lived with humility and showed so much patience during many unjust trials.

Though extremely difficult at times, the continued attempts to possess the heart of Christ will develop in us a mature sense of purpose and will magnify our ability and the ability of others to surrender all to God.

Part III
MATURE
SENSE OF PURPOSE

Chapter Seven
DISCERNMENT

I had envisioned this part of "Time Under the Cross" to be the easiest for me to elaborate on compared to the previous two parts. I can tell you it has proven to be the most difficult. While preparing my rough draft for Part III; "Mature Sense of Purpose," I came to the stark realization that I was about to penetrate my own comfort zone. To proceed with what I believed as being an "inspired" writing and to leave the structure in tact (twelve prayerfully selected chapters on topics that support the central theme—Surrenderment), I would now have to examine myself and effectively test the text. Do I really have a mature sense of purpose? Do I know how to truly discern or listen to God's will and what about my own prayer life? Are my priorities in order? The first six chapters combined did not cause me as much anguish as did Part III, namely this chapter on Discernment.

It so happens that I began writing Part III on Ash Wednesday. Go figure. For those not familiar with the Catholic Church, Ash Wednesday is the start of the Lenten season—forty days prior to

Easter Sunday. Ash Wednesday, is the day Catholic Christians place blessed ashes in the sign of the Cross on their foreheads as a symbol of humility before God. The ashes are also a symbol of mourning and sorrow at the death that sin brings into the world. As the blessed ashes are put on each person's forehead, the Priest or designated lay person says; "Turn away from sin and believe in the Gospel."

Earlier I said I was about to penetrate my own comfort zone. Using the symbolism of the smudge of ashes on the forehead for sake of parallel, I was about to tell those who someday would read this book that I believed that I had earned the right to speak out in respect to the eternal importance of being a Christian with a mature sense of purpose. That I was one who put God's will before self and walked and served with others in the effort to spread His Good News. That I recognized the risks and the regimented process needed in the continual battle against evil in our midst.

For a week leading up to me attempting the first draft of this chapter of Discernment, I felt Satan slamming me up against the ropes each time I would pick up my pen. Several times I had nearly convinced myself that this "inspired" writing would have to expire at the completion of chapter six on Patience. I could have probably retooled the structure of the book, but I would have had to live with the fact that I shorted myself, others and God because of my lack of patience and because of my fear of what I might see about myself. Point blank, I would have had to accept that I really had a lukewarm faith.

This did not set well with me when I thought about what is written in the book of Revelations where Jesus had John write down what to tell the angel of the church in Laodicea; " So, because you are lukewarm, neither hot nor cold, I will spit you out of My mouth." **1**

As I generally do, I sought counsel from a "Bible buddy" and after mentioning what I was going through; he asked me if I had thought to pray through the intersession of St. Michael the Archangel. The prayer to St. Michael is;

St. Michael the Archangel, defend me in battle. Be my protection against the wickedness and snares of the Devil. May God rebuke him, I humbly pray, and may you, O Prince of the heavenly hosts, by the Devine power of God, thrust into hell Satan, and all the evil spirits, who prowl about the world seeking the ruin of souls. Amen.

After a long discussion, my buddy and I agreed that though the pen may be mightier than the sword, in this case letting the two work together might not be a bad idea. St. Michael could weald his sword fending off Satan as I pressed on with my pen without the constant barrage of Satan's diversions and destructive intent. I committed to pray the prayer to St. Michael before picking up my pen for the remainder of this book and to say it each night throughout the forty days of Lent as a reminder of the assault from Satan that Jesus encountered during His forty days in the desert. "And He was in the wilderness forty days being tempted by Satan." **2**

I can tell you that my confidence increased dramatically and though I discerned heavily before and during this chapter on Discernment, when I picked up my pen, it had little resistance and I had the calm assurance that I was in the protective light of Christ. It was more than apparent and equally as acceptable to me that a little discomfort was a small price to pay as I served my neighbor and, like St. Michael, helped defend them in battle.

How does anyone really understand discernment? I have read on several occasions that discernment is an art. To play off of the word "art"; if I may, like art in the form of a painting, the interpretation of discernment is about as varied as are the interpretations of a gallery full of art coinsures eyeballing a Picasso.

What I found to be a common thread in my reading on the topic of discernment is that it is a way to identify God's will within the manner in which we live. Also, discernment is, or needs to be, a perpetual practice in the life of a sinner in rehab: also known as a Christian. God's will is revealed to us through the Bible especially in the teachings and the life of Jesus. However, God's will is not always easy to detect and we must be prepared and well practiced in the art of searching for what God is asking of us.

Discernment is a function of our personal relationship with God. We cannot fully discern if we do not have sound knowledge of God. Prayer, which we will spend some time looking at in Chapter 8, is a staple for knowing and loving God and is needed in heavy doses while discerning over what God has is store for us.

The more we pray for God to speak to our heart and guide us to peace and action fitting for His Kingdom, the easier it will be to distinguish God from all else. We will hear His distinct voice more often and with much more clarity when we retreat to a quite place as Jesus did so often. A place devoid of turmoil and high anxiety. This may be five minutes alone in the back yard while changing the dog's water or on a weekend retreat designed to sooth the soul. Regardless where you go or for how long, do it often and do it with the sole intent (excuse the pun) of asking for guidance and direction in your efforts to serve God with a more mature sense of purpose.

Ann Stewart, author of "With Wings of Eagles" wrote; "A purposeful life needs to be developed. You have to work it. You may not feel like you have any purpose while out of a job, sick in bed, or elderly. But, that is not true! You really do have a purpose. It's just waiting for you to tap into it and reverse the inertia into full drive."

The art of discernment requires not only prayer for guidance but also the free will to say and act on the statement; "I am going to trust and try." Praying for guidance and direction is not going to advance your position unless you engage and pursue the perceived objective. As Ann Stewart said, your purpose is "just waiting for you to tap into it."

The decision to step out and trust in times where the direction is not as clear as you would like it to be are frightening times to say the least. Your heart tells you that you are on the right path in your tireless efforts to secure work but the resounding "no" or lack of reply from the market place keeps telling your mind the exact opposite. This is very frightening. I can truly attest to how scary and confusing that situation can be. However, provided you are conditioning yourself to ask for God's will to be revealed to you and you are approaching the anticipated guidance with spiritual maturity, the end result will always be one of success in God's eye's and based on God's measure.

Below is an anonymous quote that seems quite fitting as I speak of stepping out to serve God based on His measure. I read this quote in a book written by Miles Stanford called "The Green Letters." The chapter it's found in is titled "Cultivation."

"Since the work of God is essentially spiritual, it demands spiritual people for its doing; and the measure of their spirituality will determine the measure of their value to the Lord. Because this is so, in God's mind the servant is more than the work. If we are going to come truly into the hands of God for His purpose, then we shall be dealt with by Him in such a way as to continually increase our spiritual measure. Not our interest in Christian work; our energies, enthusiasm, ambitions, or abilities; not our academic qualification, or anything that we are in ourselves, but simply our spiritual life is the basis of the beginning and growth of our service to God. Even the work, when we are in it, is used by Him to increase our spiritual measure" (Anon.).

We Christians are called to grow, to mature, in the knowledge of Jesus. As discussed in chapters two and three (knowledge / understanding) scripture is where we can really get to know the full breadth of God's love and His plans for us. The New Testament alone is packed full of many signs of Christ's works and His sovereign power. Jesus practiced discernment each time He went to be alone with His Father.

Following the feeding of the five thousand and just before walking on the water on His way to Gennesaret, Jesus retreated to the mountain side. "He went up on the mountain by Himself to pray." **3**

Jesus went into the desert for forty days immediately following Him having been baptized in water by John the Baptist and having received the Holy Spirit from God along side the Jordan River. "And He was in the wilderness forty days being tempted by Satan." **4**

Shortly after Jesus' Triumphal Entry into Jerusalem (where He drove out from the Temple area "money changers" and those selling doves), one evening He left the Disciples and the crowds to be alone. "And leaving them, He went out of the city of Bethany, and there He spent the night." **5**

Just before His Passion and on the night of Passover, Jesus went to a quite place three separate times within the Garden of Gethsemane. "He left them *(Peter, James and his brother John)* and withdrew again and prayed a third time, saying the same thing again"…"My Father, if it is not possible that this cup pass without My drinking it, Your will be done!." **6**

Even at the young age of twelve, Christ broke from His family's caravan and stayed at the Temple in Jerusalem. "Then, after three days they (Mary and Joseph) found Him in the temple, sitting in the midst of the teachers, both listening and asking questions."

"He went…to Nazareth, and He continued in subjection to them…increasing in wisdom and stature, and in favor with God and men." **7**

Jesus repeatedly made an "all out" effort to identify God's will within the manner in which He lived. Jesus lived to know and serve God. We may say; "Well, yeah, He is God's Son. They are one in the same." Christ did dwell among us. "And the Word became flesh, and dwelt among us." **8** He was without sin, no doubt, but He was still human. Jesus worked really hard to cultivate discernment and He tirelessly avoided deception.

If we want a matured sense of purpose in our lives and if we want to strive to identify God's will for us, we have got to dig deep and cultivate discernment as Jesus did. Again, as Ann Stewart put it: "you have to work it."

If discernment is an art, then we need to become the artisan. We must train ourselves to act in such a manner that helps prevent us from falling prey to a variety of deceptive lures bombarding our senses every day. We must become savvy and relentless in our efforts to prevent the mind set of false promise from defusing the crystal clear and long view available through the loving eyes of Christ.

Whether we think we are on top of the world or buried under heaps of what the world throws upon us, we must have an internal sounding system that alerts us to these deceptions. The practice of discernment is just that; a method where we can silence the world, reflect on the Word and hear the sound of God's quiet whisper. The "here and now" culture of this world is embedded in our minds. Going to the Word, praying and quietly listening to God is how we can best sort out and keep focus on our priorities. We must continue to work to transform ourselves and grow in our desire and knowledge of what God has planned for us to do in and for His glory.

St. Paul writes in his address to the Roman's; "Do not conform yourselves to this age but be transformed by the renewal of your mind, that you may discern what is the will of God, what is good and pleasing and perfect." **9** Regardless what stage we are at in our spiritual maturity, we all must continue to mature ourselves with knowledge and silence our wants while listening for what we need to have in our life for the sake of pleasing God. In doing this, we will train ourselves in the art of discernment and despite the evil in our midst, we will be successful in our ability to hear and to act on God's calling while avoiding what leads us to sin.

Don't be alarmed or put out if the process takes longer than you were thinking it would. If we push for an answer it might not be the one God wanted us to hear. What may feel like a slow bake may be the exact time in the oven we needed to really get our attention for both what is in balance in our lives and what is out of balance in our lives. When I speak of balance, I am referring to the balance between what we think we want and what God is telling us.

Focus on Jesus Christ as the fulcrum (one that supplies capability for action) as you discern of matters pertaining to achieving balance in your Christian life. Through the Holy Spirit, He will guide you to add or take away those elements necessary to create perfect balance between your wants and God's will.

When things become a little stagnate in our life and no answers are coming our way, even though we trust and we are trying to discern, we are often tempted to quit or go create a desirable outcome ourselves. That temptation is not from God. When this happens we need to tough it out and surrender the fear, not surrender to the fear. God will send us wisdom and many other gifts of the Holy Spirit to see us through.

Earlier I said that praying for guidance and direction is not going to advance your position unless you engage and pursue the perceived objective. This statement could send mixed signals. On one hand "engage and pursue" may sound like taking control for selfish reasons. One the other hand, "engage and pursue" may sound like taking action based on what you hear in your heart. The latter is what is needed in combination with prayers for guidance.

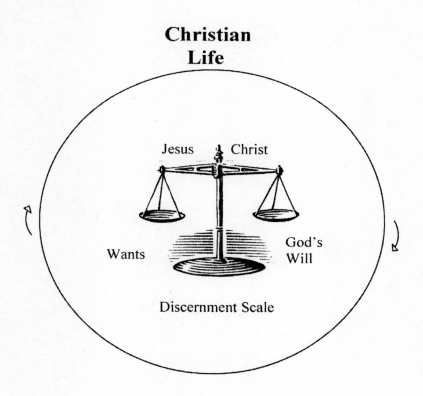

God will most likely not lay out a time line and critical path styled action plan. However, He will give us the tools to proceed and He will show us signs along the way that reaffirm the decisions we make. We will see God's hand at work. He will lead us as we walk and the view ahead will become crystal clear. We will have heard God's quite whisper and our sense of purpose for acting in faith will be more matured than ever before.

"Let us be ashamed to be caught up by worthless imaginings, for at the time of prayer we speak to the great King."—St. Francis

Chapter Eight
PRAYER

One Friday afternoon about eight years after Crickett and I were married, we were playing cards at my parent's home. My Dad said how he wished we could just take off and drive to Lake Charles, LA (approximately 300 miles from Corpus Christi, TX) and play Texas Hold'em aboard one of the river boat casinos in the area. On a whim, we arranged for a close family friend to baby sit our daughters for the night and into the next day. Within seven hours we were playing poker at a "live" table. Several hours and several dollars later, we retired to the room we were to share during the few hours we had planned to sleep.

It was around 4AM once everyone had gotten ready for bed. The room was dark and quiet. My Mom knelt next to her side of the bed that she and Dad were sharing. Mom lifted her hands ever so slightly and bowed her head. About that time, from the dark silence of the room came these words; "Wilma, if I've told you once I've told you a thousand times, you don't have to bow and pay homage to me before you come to bed." It was my Dad's voice we heard.

Following much laughter, Mom returned to her nightly prayer and concluded aloud asking God to please give Raymond (my Dad) just one more chance to get into Heaven.

I mentioned in the Forward of this book how my Mom armed our family with her profound faith and that my prayer life is mainly attributed to Mom. Dad and Mom both taught us how to pray and prayed with us quite often. However, it was my Mom who I recall always praying for others and her own. When an ambulance would go by with its siren on; "Say a prayer for the person inside and their family." Dinner would be piping hot and on the table while our forks were tightly gripped and aimed at pre-selected potatoes; "You kids stop. Let's pray first."

A devout Christian is likely to have a well founded knowledge, appreciation and personalized method for prayer. It goes without saying that the Bible references prayer on nearly every page. Those who truly appreciate the value gained from prayer may not all have an aggressive appetite for reading the Bible, but I am very confident they have been deeply enriched by the primary teaching and inspirational accounts of faith, hope and love found throughout the Bible.

It was 1791 AD before the First Family Bible was printed in America. **1** Not until the late 1800's was the Bible readily available to the average person. Until that time, fellow Christians were sharing Bible stories and practical methods of worship to those hungry for the Word of God. These devout disciples of Christ, whether the 16th century Franciscan Friars teaching the Nahua Indians in Central Mexico or a 19th century trail boss sharing Bible stories with his wranglers along the Chisholm Trail; both were praying in their own right. They were taking their knowledge and understanding of the Word and were spreading it to others out of love for God and for neighbor.

Prayer, in general terms, is when we apply our minds toward God's Divinity. It is when we seek God's sovereign power for direction and for assistance to achieve His will during our walk with Him. Prayer is the act where the will of God is brought into correspondence with the free will of the one doing the praying. The object of prayer is not to change the will of God, but to secure for ourselves, and for others, blessings that God is already willing to grant. Through prayer we can be in union with God and we can open a dialog that provides insight and direction to how we can better serve Him. When we just simply praise God for being God and thank Him for everything from general gifts of sun, rain, breeze, etc. to particular gifts such as a bad cold that has gotten better or a loved one having called us on a given day, we too are praying to our Great Provider.

Four types of prayer are mentioned in 1 Timothy 2:1, 3; "I ask that supplications, praise, petitions, and thanksgivings be offered for everyone. This is good and pleasing to God our savior."

Prayer of Supplication. This type of prayer is that of needs, results and desires.

Prayer of Praise. This type of prayer involves worship/devotional adoration, exhalation and praise to God.

Prayer of Intercession. This type of prayer lifts the burdens and needs of others to God.

Prayer of Thanksgiving. This type of prayer is the offering of thanks to God because of who He is as well as what He has done.

Several styles or methods of prayer have been practiced for centuries:

Prayer of the heart—Repeating a prayer word or phrase ("Jesus" or "I trust in You") continuously and while synchronizing it with your breathing.

Centering prayer or Contemplative prayer—The discipline of resting in God and allowing your heart to hear God's whisper.

Lectio Divina (Sacred Readings)—selecting a scripture you are drawn to and slowly reading it several times while trying to obtain how it relates to you personally.

An excellent source for an in depth explanation of these and many others forms of prayer can be found in the book; "Praying with Friends and Enemies: Intercessory Prayer" written by the Rev. Jan Vennard. **2**

Part of my Catholic Christian up bringing included the reciting and memorization of several traditional prayers such as; The Lord's Prayer, Hail Mary, Glory Be and the Apostles Creed. These prayers each cover some of the reasons we pray as mentioned earlier. "Our Father who art in Heaven, Hollowed be Thy name..." and "Glory be to the Father, the Son and the Holy Spirit..." are forms of praise. "I believe in one God, the Father almighty, Creator of Heaven and earth..." is a profession of faith.

Another style or method of prayer is spontaneous prayer. It was not until I really began to read the Bible and various spiritual books and articles that I obtained an appreciation for this type of prayer. As I was growing up, my Protestant friends and their families would prayer before their meal a little differently than we did within our family. Also, when I would attend a wake service, the pastor or minister would pray aloud, free style. As I matured in my faith, it became comfortable and somewhat exhilarating to say aloud what was alive in my heart.

Spontaneous prayer does not have to be formal. It can be a creative thought that simply reflects our love for God and our need and desire to have Him in our life. King David, in the book of Psalms, prayed spontaneously and it is as if he was holding nothing back.

Prayer is an intimate expression covering our desires, beliefs and broad based feelings toward God. Whether expressed in private or in public; aloud or in our mind, the expression is still a personal connection between you and God. Therefore, the style you select should be one you feel best brings God's will into correspondence with your own.

When we genuinely pray, we tend to humble ourselves in that we are admitting our dependence and our neediness. We too are acknowledging God's awesome power, goodness and Divine presence. A good way to start off a prayer is to announce our weakness and sinful nature followed by acknowledging His awesome power. Whether you proceed with select prayers you have grown accustom to, break into a spontaneous discourse that best presents your innermost feelings or sit silently while breathing in Christ and breathing out crisis, know that God hears you. Recall in the book of John where the man, once blind, said to the Pharisees; "We know that God does not listen to sinners, but if one is devout and does His will, He hears him." **3**

"Networking" is a term frequently used in business circles. Networking is "a supportive system of sharing information and services among individuals and groups having a common interest." **4** What is essential when networking is that the effort put into the action be genuine and continuous. If we genuinely and continuously go to God in prayer, He will respond in grace and many caring and capable people from all walks of life will become apparent to us as either ones to serve our needs or ones to be served in their time of need.

God answers all of our prayers. He does hear us. We must choose to respond selflessly in faith despite our own wanton expectations and rely on the tender love of God to provide in such a way that best supports His will.

Taking the concept of networking a little further in respect to prayer, the Internet is proving to be an excellent tool for networking with others requesting for prayers. Prayer chains are being established, formally and informally, throughout the world. One person cries out to another for prayer before the surgery of her daughter and within minutes, the request has exponentially grown and is immediately on the minds and in the hearts of hundreds of people who in turn petition the need of their neighbor before God.

Despite the method of prayer we choose and whether we send our prayer to God alone or share it with others, we need not loose sight that prayer is necessary for salvation. Throughout the Gospels, Jesus practices and speaks of prayer in most every discourse or teaching. "Ask and it will be given to you; seek and you will find; knock and the door will be opened to you." **5** "Persevere in prayer, being watchful in it with thanksgiving." **6** "Without prayer, we cannot resist temptation, nor obtain God's grace, nor grow and persevere in God's grace." **7**

In the time soon after the death and resurrection of Jesus, Christians believed that the second coming of Christ was weeks or months away. They took the words of St. Paul; "pray unceasingly," **8** very seriously because many believed salvation and the end of the world, as they knew it, was about to knock on their door.

As was for the early Christians, the same is true for us in that we know Christ will come again and we are aware that we "do not know when the appointed time will come." **9** To "pray unceasingly," for me, is to have my heart open to hear God and to be heard by God. There are going to be those times when we close our hearts to God. Those times can be frequent for me when I want things my way. It is important that we make the effort to go to or go back to God often. When we are being true about our sinfulness and obedient to His commandments, we know when it is necessary to pray. It might be when we feel the overwhelming need to give praise or when we want to give thanksgiving for what we have or do not have. It might be in petition for a specific need or to ask for His wisdom to keep us on the sinless path home.

Prayer is a great resource. It can bring about miraculous results if approached with a mind poised to disconnect from the hustle and bustle of time eaters and deadlines and is centered with a heart that is conditioned to absorb the nurturing guidance and love God is so ready to reveal. Silence is the language of God.

As we endure in prayer, we will develop a deeper and more intimate relationship with God. Though God's love for us is intense and unconditional, through prayer we can gain a better appreciation for His love of us while showing appreciation to Him in the form of praise or thanksgiving or by selflessly petitioning for the needs of others.

Try to become a prayer warrior with and for others. As does any "warrior," we too must first put on our armor. In this case, we must wear the armor of the Word. St. Paul said; "Put on the armor of God, that you may be able to stand against the wiles of the devil." **10** Next, we must pray fervently for God's grace to penetrate the heart, soul and mind of all believers and non-believers alike.

Praying for a child with cancer is much easier than praying for the cashier who greets you with an attitude saying; "yeah, how can I help ya?" Both those that are defenseless and those that are contemptible deserve God's grace. I just labeled the cashier as contemptible based on six words spoken and my perception of the tone used. Maybe this person is a parent with a young child in a children's hospital battling cancer. We never know what impact our prayers will have, but we do know that without a heart trained on penetrating the hearts of others, we will have chose to not do as St. Paul asked; "pray unceasingly."

Praying together is such a good way to stay active in our prayer life. Those we pray with are struggling with time issues, problems and doubts just like us. The collective effort not only invokes the Holy Spirit; "Where two or three have gathered in My name, I am there in their midst," **11** it also allows you to not feel isolated in your personal trials. If you are beginning to feel like you have nothing to pray for in your own life, no doubt you will leave your prayer session with loads of reasons to pray.

A well grounded and enthusiastic prayer life will play a defining roll as you mature spiritually and you will become all the more aware of your purpose in life and in the lives of others.

I wish to close this chapter on Prayer with a prayer for peace written by the late Pope John Paul II.

"Lord Jesus Christ, who are called the Prince of Peace, who are yourself our peace and reconciliation, who so often said, 'Peace to you', grant us peace. Make all men and women witnesses of truth, justice, and brotherly love. Banish from their hearts whatever might endanger peace. Enlighten our rulers that they may guarantee and defend the great gift of peace. May all peoples on the earth become as brothers and sisters. May longed-for peace blossom forth and reign always over us all. Amen."

"Seek first His kingdom and His righteousness." Matthew
6:33

Chapter Nine
PRIORITIES

Visualize yourself and your family in a row boat out in the middle
of a large isolated lake. Suddenly you hear a creaking sound
followed by a loud crack and without hardly any notice at all, your
day, once filled with peace and relaxation, is now filled with panic
and uncertainty; not to mention a tremendous amount of water both
inside and outside of your boat.

Can you picture this situation? Are you in the boat and can you
feel the water rising under your feet? Now, let me ask you two more
questions. First, have your priorities changed due to the turn of
events? Second, what are your priorities now?

I am sure that if we were sitting together addressing these
questions in a small group, but not in a boat, the latter would have
much variance and no doubt our exchange of ideas would be lively.
As for the first question; "have your priorities changed due to the turn
of events?" I imagine we would all agree on a resounding; "YES!"

When we say "yes" to God, our priorities change in a big way too.
We most likely have had an awakening or an epiphany of sorts that
brought on the call to discern and pray for guidance. The events and

the timing might not have been as dramatic and immediate as those on the boat but nonetheless, in that special moment, God gains our attention and we have a heightened awareness for the need to address the prospect of change and redirection in our spiritual lives.

So what do you say? Let's get our feet wet and delve into the priorities pertaining to fully surrendering to God and allowing Him to guide our actions as we set our sights on salvation. Don't worry about the sinking feeling you might have—God will keep you afloat.

In 1 John 2:15-17 we read; "Do not love the world or things of the world…the world passes away…but he who does the will of God abides forever." I chose this scripture for starters because on first pass, it sounds so anti "now." It's a lot like what Jesus said in Luke 14:33 that we covered in chapter two on Knowledge; "Any of you who do not give up everything he has cannot be My Disciple." Recall me sharing how if you were like me, you might have thought; "I love you God, but I'm confused. I have a life and I **am** trying. God, you did give me the desire and ability to live out this life, didn't you?"

The confusing and scary part about surrendering to and following God is that it requires change. It challenges our comfort zones. If what we are doing "now" feels comfortable, then change from our norm is going to usher in doubt and we are going to resist with thoughts or statements similar to how we did as defiant teenagers whenever our parents asked us to do things their way. "Ah Dad, you are always against me having fun and doing things my way."

"Mom, can you ask anything more ridiculous or impossible than that?"

I said a moment ago that the first time you read 1 John 2:15-17 it sounded so anti "now." Let's read it again; "Do not love the world or things of the world…the world passes away…but he who does the will of God *abides* forever." I took this passage and used the form of prayer; Lectio Divina (Sacred Readings). I slowly read it several times and tried to really hear what it was saying to me in the context of priorities. I finally got it.

What I was getting caught up in was the directive "do not." What I was over looking was the word "abides." I looked to see how this word was used in several other books of the Bible and from what I could gather, the word "abide" means to wait on, to trust in, the Lord while bearing spiritual fruit. "Just as the Father has loved Me, I have also loved you; *abide* in My love." 1 To abide is not to sit on our laurels with knowledge of His Word while refraining from putting the Word into works. To abide is not striving to achieve something in a reckless manner without a sense of purpose or without a plan. To abide is to rely on Jesus and to allow the Holy Spirit to guide you to and through God's will.

If we are abiding; if we are enduring the trials here on Earth by using the gifts of the Holy Spirit (wisdom, understanding, knowledge, counsel, fortitude, piety and fear of the Lord) then we will in turn be rewarded fruits from the same Spirit. Among these fruits are; charity, joy, peace, patience, goodness, modesty. 2 If we apply these gifts out of true love of God (Agape) the "things of the world" will still have their place and will provide enjoyment and sustenance but they will not interfere with the will of God. It is here that we will both produce and be rewarded "fruit" and it is here when we begin to abide; both on Earth and "forever."

We can all agree that there is an evil undertow lurking at every bend, both in the depths and the shallows of our lives, looking for any weakness that can be manipulated and therefore creating a diversion of our well intended motives. The more certain we are about our present status in our spiritual journey; where we intend to ultimately be and how we will achieve getting there, the more likely it is that major attempts will be made to grossly distract us from obtaining our goal, our eternal end. Satan and his evil spirits will trip you, trick you and trump you throughout your life. As our good works increase,

Satan is going to intensify his efforts to turn us from God and as sinners we, at times, are going to turn.

The key is to turn back to God. With our priorities in good order, we can quickly regain our footing when we slip away from God. God and the things of God should be our first priority. We are given this instruction in the first three commandments of the ten commandments. First commandment—"I, the LORD, am your God...you shall not have other gods besides me." **3** Second commandment—"You shall not take the name of the Lord, your God, in vain." **4** Third commandment—"Take care to keep holy the Sabbath day. Remember the Sabbath and keep it holy." **5** Jesus also teaches us that God should be our first priority when he said; "You shall love the Lord your God with all your heart and with all your soul and all your mind and with all of your strength." **6**

God put us first by creating us in His Divine image and giving us dominion over all living things. God makes certain that we are blessed with an overwhelming abundance of such a variety of gifts in our lives. The most evident gift of all that so lovingly reminds us that we are priority one in God's eyes is the gift of His only son, Jesus.

If we can just remain mindful of all that God does for us, then it is much easier to want to show our gratitude, love and respect by emulating Christ and serving/loving others. "You shall love your neighbor as yourself." **7** Also, having the consistent reminder of how blessed and loved we are will motivate us to practice what Jesus said; "It is more blessed to give than to receive."**8**

"To give" leads us to the remaining priorities. To give what? To give of your entire self out of love by sharing your gifts of time, talent and treasure. The exact allocation of these gifts is very personal. No one person call tell you exactly how, where and how much of each you should delve out. However, I think it is fair to say that as we pray for Wisdom, the Holy Spirit will help us recognize our gifts and guide us to use them according to His will.

No doubt we will occasionally be tempted by Satan, but as we prayerfully try to maintain a good balance in our Christian life between our "wants" and "God's will" (recall the discernment scale in chapter 7), we will make calm and clear judgments as how to proceed. We will be at peace as we give necessary attention to family, work, church and relaxation.

Prioritization of our gifts in respect to knowing, loving and serving God should be as devoid of human measure and preconceived notions as possible. I am not saying we should not schedule our time, budget our money or have, in place, a game plan of sorts. What I am saying is we should be very open to being guided by the hands of God for His purpose. As mentioned in chapter 7, as long as we are conditioning ourselves to ask for God's will to be revealed to us and we are approaching the anticipated guidance with spiritual maturity, the end result will be one of success in God's eyes and will be reflective of our spiritual measure and not that of our human measure.

This might be a good time to survey yourself in respect to where the following areas of focus rank in your life. If you are up to it, go get a piece of paper and a pencil and jot down the following six interests; recreation, family, God, work, money and self. Now, rank these in order of their priority in your life. This is a tough thing to do so if you are thinking of just skipping this exercise for now, that's okay. Just please consider coming back to it when you hear God whispering to you about where He ranks in your life.

If you chose to do the ranking of priorities, now circle the top three of the six interests. This is a pretty good indication as to where you allocate the majority of your blessed gifted of time, talent and treasure.

I have included in the notes and resources segment of this book a list of scripture references you may wish to read. They were selected for their individual relevance to the gifts of time, talent and treasure. **9**

Consider doing one more thing. Take a moment following the completion of this paragraph and close your eyes and begin to breathe slowly and deeply. Breathe Christ in and crisis out. Ask the Holy Spirit to talk to your heart about your priorities. Even if you chose not to do the above exercise, still consider letting the Holy Spirit talk to you.

Go ahead, I'll wait for you. Matter of fact, I am going to set my pen down and do the same right this minute.

Earlier in this chapter I said that your priorities are personal and that no one can tell you exactly where, how and how much of each of your gifts should be expensed. It is my prayer that the exercise and or the act of you having spent a little time with the Holy Spirit will shed some light on where to focus your own light—the light of Christ from within you.

I am sure you have read or heard the passage from the book of Matthew about the lamp and the bushel basket. I think this Bible quote is a good one to meditate on when discerning about priorities and what we are doing with our blessed gifts. "Nor does anyone light a lamp and put it under a basket, but on the lamp stand, and it gives light to all who are in the house." **10**

We should try to focus on being spiritual in all of our actions, regardless of our vocation in life. We can rest assured God will help us track our progress and He will communicate back to our hearts, in His time. Matter of fact, He just did as we asked Him to talk to us about priorities.

A devout spiritual lifestyle makes navigating through all trials and triumphs much more rewarding and the prize of Heaven will shine before you as a beacon even in the thickest blanket of fog. The awareness of God being the absolute source of all that you are and all that you will achieve in His light is where you can find much peace today and each day forward.

We are about to conclude Part III; "Mature Sense of Purpose." I want to emphasize the importance and interconnection of; Discernment, Prayer and Priorities. While praying about how I could best emphasize this, I remembered having read an article within a newsletter called "A Look in the Mirror." The article was written by Patrick Morley and was titled "How to order your priorities." Mr. Morley referenced a passage in the book of Luke to show how Jesus made decisions based on His priorities. It was in this passage that I felt I could best emphasize the importance and interconnection of the three theme support topics within this part of "Time Under the Cross."

"At daybreak, Jesus left and went to a deserted place. The crowds went looking for Him, and when they came to Him, they tried to prevent Him from leaving them. But He said to them, 'To the other towns also I must proclaim the good news of the kingdom of God, because for this purpose I have been sent'." **11**

In this passage, we have yet another great example of Jesus, human like each of us, staying true to His daily regiment and getting away to let God whisper to His heart. Jesus disciplined Himself to nurture His personal relationship with God the Father. He consistently stepped out, away from the worldly distractions, and listened for God's will to be revealed to Him. Not in an audible or written "To Do" list but in a soothing and soaking inner voice that His heart longed to hear.

Jesus had a well founded knowledge and appreciation of the Word of God and a personalized method for prayer. I am sure while growing up in Nazareth He had the best of examples of others who prayed with all of their heart. People such as His mother Mary, Joseph, His cousin John the Baptist and many other family members and friends who shared His love and devotion for God.

Lastly, Jesus prioritized. He put God first and He knew when it was time to respond to God's call. This is why He was able to tell the people; whom He loved so dearly that were eager to keep Him from leaving; "I must preach the good news...because for this purpose I was sent." You too are called to preach the Good News throughout our daily lives. Being attentive to the availability and distribution of our time, talent and treasure (through dutiful prioritization) you will surely get the Good News out to the good people waiting and yearning to experience God through your labor of love.

Part IV
DETERMINED WILL

Chapter Ten
JOYFUL SPIRIT

Throughout this book, I have made several references of the gifts and the fruits of the Holy Spirit. Among the fruits of the Holy Spirits is "Joy." The fruit of "joy" just like the fruit of "charity," which I will expand upon in Chapter 11 as Christian Action, is a byproduct of the seven gifts of the Holy Spirit. The gifts of the Spirit come to us from the Holy Spirit Himself. We didn't have to earn them; we can't give them back; they are ours forever. To quote a life long friend of mine following me having said that I will remain married to Crickett forever, he replied with a pondering yet playful tone in his voice; "Wow, forever; now that's a long time."

We all have these gifts available to us forever. Now, whether we acknowledge the gifts of the Holy Spirit, and strive to produce their intended fruit, is entirely left for our choosing. However, if we do acknowledge the gifts of the Holy Spirit (wisdom, understanding, knowledge, counsel, fortitude, piety and fear of the Lord) and apply them throughout our lives, we will produce an abundance of fruit. As

Jesus said in the book of John; "Amen, amen, I say to you, unless a grain of wheat falls to the ground and dies, it remains just a grain of wheat; but if it dies, it produces much fruit."**1**

Have you ever toiled from early spring through mid to late summer with a garden? Maybe you started with small tomato plants. You prepped the soil, protected the plants from the wind, most insects and the occasional soccer ball that seemed to always mistake the garden for the goal.

Perhaps you walked away with shoulders drooping one summer evening thinking you had better acquire a taste for weeds. When you returned the next day, to your amazement you were graced with the fruit of your labor, the product of your knowledge and fortitude. You were determined to take what you had available to you and preserver; and you did.

Do you remember the unbridled joy you felt when you saw dots of red among a backdrop of green. That's the type of joy God wants each and every one of His children to have in their hearts at all times. The book of James reminds us of this with; "Consider it all joy, my brothers, when you encounter various trials, for you know that the testing of your faith produces perseverance."

God wants us to have a joyful spirit from the time we wake in the morning until the time we retire in the evening. God wants us to rejoice in His love. He is pure love and, remember, we were created in His image. The key nutrient to joy is love.

In the book of Ephesians, Paul commanded that all Christians be "filled with the Spirit." **3** What does "be filled with the Spirit" really mean? I can only surmise that it relates to the fruits produced from the gifts of the same Spirit. We all know the feeling of excitement and happiness we experience when a bride and groom share their wedding vows or when a new born baby smiles and coos or when we revel over the fact that we get to have a fresh tomato sandwich and not one made with weeds.

To be "filled with the Spirit" is to submit entirely, to surrender, to the love and protection of God and to allow Him to penetrate every pore of your being. When you have a minute, I suggest you read Ephesians chapter 5 in its entirety. Paul goes to great lengths in detailing what the people of Ephesus and all Christians should displace in order to be "filled with the Spirit."

I keep a two inch by two inch "stick-em" on the glass portion of the dashboard of my truck that covers my gas gauge. It is tattered and torn and no longer has much "stick" left to it. What is written on the faded yellow paper are these words; "I offer to You Lord all that I have, all that I am, all that I aspire to be—'Jesus, I trust in You'." I lift this note up when I get in my truck so to see if I am near "F" or "E." I also read it each time for the sake of reconfirming my determined will to remain "f"illed with the Holy Spirit and to not allow myself to be "e"mptied of the promises and the gifts from Christ because of selfishness or the lack of faith.

I once read that joy is "the feeling of grinning on the inside." To keep this inner grin alive throughout our day and throughout our life, we are required to work hard to "erase from our minds all hostility, resentment, fear and insecurity. If we can do this, we will always be able to live in and share true joy." **4**

Nothing comes easy as we all know. To erase all hostility, resentment, fear and insecurity from our minds sounds like a tall order; one that is nearly impossible. But not for God, because "with God all things are possible." **5** Let's not forget that God gave us Jesus. Jesus gave us life through His death and resurrection and we now live with the gifts of the Holy Spirit that are "qualities infused into our soul by the Holy Spirit." **6** The gifts of the Holy Spirit are ours and if we surrender fully to God and respond to His call with a determined will, we can continuously improve in faith and erase these obstacles through the application of the subsequent fruits. We can apply these fruits to benefit ourselves and to benefit our neighbors—both the friendly ones and those that are not so friendly.

Neither joy nor any of the fruits of the Holy Spirit can eradicate sin while we are here on Earth. As long as we are in the flesh, we continue to sin and be subject to the affects of sin itself. Suffering has been a part of the human experience since the first Covenant was broken by Adam and Eve. There are many events that crop up in our lives that we may never truly understand as to why we are subjected to them. We might even find ourselves doubting God at times because we feel in our hearts that we are living in accordance to His will yet we are being unfairly bombarded by events that are not pleasant by human measure.

Maybe we lost our job, lost a family member, were wrongfully accused of something or maybe we fell and broke an arm. Any one of these events is definitely not on anyone's "favorite things" list. However, if we "consider it all joy" and continue to walk in, with and through Christ, there will be no room in our mind or in our heart for anything other than that of forgiveness, acceptance and peace.

For those of you who may have friends or family members who are terminally ill or who may be ill yourselves, let me first extend my heart and my prayers to each and every one of you. I recently stood at the bedside of a dear friend who would go home to God just days later. This friend was experiencing unbearable physical pain despite the many pain medications his doctors were prescribing. Though his body was responding to pain, I saw no pain in his eyes. Have you ever noticed that when you have the opportunity to look into the eyes of someone who is terminally ill but is living for Christ, that its as if you can see straight to their soul? For a split second or two you sense peace radiating from them. It's as if they are communicating that even though they are broken in flesh there are no obstacles between them and God.

It is my belief that these dear souls are spiritually at peace even though they are obviously in much physical pain. They have committed themselves to utilize the gifts of the Holy Spirit, namely long suffering (patient endurance of pain or unhappiness), **7** as a means of showing their love for God. Furthermore, I am convinced that their selfless act of enduring this form of suffering paves the way for others to experience the redeeming love of Christ. Maybe its the caregiver on the same wing of the hospital who had fallen away from God because of the never ending stream of illness and death but now feels a renewed sense of purpose and compassion for those in need. Maybe it's a pregnant teenage girl on her way for an abortion who in a split second feels she should pull into the Church she just passed but really doesn't know why.

You know from chapter 6 that I'm a betting man. I would wager that you have either sung or hummed the tone of the song "Joyful, Joyful, We Adore Thee." But have you really sat and soaked on the lyrics, especially those of the first verse.

Joyful, joyful, (Lord) we adore Thee, God of glory, Lord of love; hearts unfold like flow'rs (flowers) before Thee, opening to the sun above.

Melt the clouds of sin and sadness; drive the dark of doubt away.

Giver of immortal gladness, fill us with the light of day!

Henry van Dyke wrote these lyrics in 1907 and the tune it is sung to is that of Beethoven's "Ode to Joy." **8** He was a very accomplished man who walked in the light of Christ. Notice that Mr. van Dyke chose "joy," a fruit of the Spirit, to use while giving praise to God. Also, see how he makes a point to reference the nourishment, warmth and brilliant light available to us in God's love. To write with such expression is a blessing in and of itself; however, such talent seems to reach full maturity when both gifts and fruits of the Holy Spirit accompany one's labor of love.

My family attends Sunday Mass together and afterwards we always try to go have breakfast at a Texas based restaurant chain named "Whataburger." Not only is the food really good, the acoustics must be too. We often have people stop by our table and let us know how they were pleasantly moved by something they overheard one of our daughters say about an experience at Mass or that of a kind tone used by one of them while all three were each trying to be first in line at the drink dispenser. An older couple took time one morning to say; "It's such a joy to hear and see your family praying together before your meal." I am sure if they had listened a little closer they would have also heard; "take another one of my fries and you loose an arm."

We, like many Christians, commune in private and in public with no pretentious intent. We just strive to remain Christ-centered. We work on knowing, loving and serving God as fully as we possibly can while dealing with the twists and turns, the bumps and bruises and the many joyful moments that God provides for us each and every day.

As we, discerning Christians, grow stronger in faith each day, we will be recognized as being or having a joyful spirit. The recognition that will count the most, however, is our own internal recognition. Similar to that of the top need (self actualization) in Abraham Maslow's Hierarchy of Needs model, **9** internal or individualized recognition of having a joyful spirit is very rewarding and significant enough proof that we are on the right tract in terms of helping accomplish God's will.

Our spiritual hearing will get significantly better and we will be "self actualized" and satisfied when we hear God whispering to our heart with loving reassurance and with new challenges intended to further our growth and service.

Just as I said in chapter 7 of Discernment where "we must have an internal sounding system that alerts us of the deceptive lures that bombard our senses everyday," we too must rely on a similar sounding system that is calibrated to pick up on the nuances of God's acceptance and great appreciation for our loving behaviors, our service and our suffering. There is no doubt it feels great to have others we care for validate our good behaviors. However, if we only listen for and respond to this means of acceptance and validation, we will find ourselves disillusioned when the praise is lacking and our motives will begin to shift from selfless to selfish.

Who in your life do you perceive as the quintessential spirit of joy? Really give this question some serious thought. Do not limit yourself to only those in your family or an Elder in your Church. Think through a variety of people who; are presently in your life, have since passed away and or those who only have graced you with their presence for a brief moment.

I ask this question and challenge you to dig deep because we each have been blessed with so many great examples of Christianity through the words and actions of men and women who many times go unnoticed. I don't mean unnoticed in that we didn't or don't acknowledge them or thank them, but more so that we may have overlooked how they can be remembered and utilized as an excellent benchmark for us as we work to fill our spiritual life with joy.

If you have pondered the above question and are coming up with several people who are great examples of a joyful spirit, be sure to thank God and say a prayer for these people who through their Christ like demeanor selflessly acted out of kindness to and for you.

I sat and thought through my life and listed those who I consider as joyful spirits. The list was rather long but the common thread seemed to be that each of these joy filled people had/have the following characteristics:

Forever Thankful

Realistically Optimistic

Awestruck by God's Every Creation

Dedication to Prayer

Tireless Service to Those in Need

In preparation of Time Under the Cross, I made it a point to review books I had once read. Also, I chose to read a few more select books and articles throughout the process. It came to my mind that the authors of these books and the people some authors wrote about could have easily topped my "joyful spirit" list. Reason being, the previously listed characteristics, demonstrated throughout their lives, were evident. Also, their trials, tribulations and successes deeply moved me and have had a profound effect on me as a joyful spirit—a joyful spirit in training, that is.

The person I chose as being my benchmark for a joyful spirit, second only to Jesus, is a wonderful lady we call Janet. She is the grandmother to a life long friend of my daughter Randi. My family was graced by the acquaintance of this "lady" several years ago. At first we addressed her by her last name, led with the prefix of "Mrs.," of course. She was quick to warmly say; "Oh, no dear, please call me Janet. That is what my friends call me."

We communicate often with Janet via E-mail and letters and we see her a couple times a year as she travels throughout the US visiting her children and grandchildren. All visits with Janet are filled with stories and living examples of a person who loves Christ, loves life and lives in Christ's love.

I recently wrote Janet and told her I was writing this book. I also asked her to pray for the daughter of one of my friends who had been badly injured in an auto accident. Janet's reply was a little more delayed than usual and I became concerned. I did receive a reply and within it I found that even as she was writing, she was extremely ill. To illustrate why Janet is the benchmark of a "joyful spirit" for me, I wish to share with you Janet's reply.

Dear Ron—

Forgive my delay in replying—I have been struggling with a severe respiratory infection for the last month and a half or longer—am so weak—even now—

And so my thoughts on the subject of your new-found "calling" will have to wait a bit. I want to be able to say what is really in my heart—and at the moment it is taking all of my energy to simply sit upright at the computer....

I'm on the mend—if ever so slowly—but I just can't stay out of bed or off the couch for long. I would appreciate your prayers.

I'm very excited about your new venture—and I know that it could only be a nudge from God, as this sort of thing always is....

Forgive me for being so self-centered at the moment. In times like this, all of our strong faith seems a far-distant memory—Prayer is impossible—only leaning into the heart of God will do....

I will write soon. My prayers are with you—and with the young woman who has suffered such severe injuries - and All involved in what must have been a terrible accident. (It makes me so ashamed of my complaints....)

My love to all the family—pcangel (Janet)

As mentioned earlier, love is a key nutrient and ingredient for joy. If we remain centered in Christ's love, we will produce much joy and our actions are likely to inspire others to emulate Christ because of our selfless and reflective example.

"What does it profit, my brethren, if a man says he has faith but has not works?" (James 2:14)

Chapter Eleven
CHRISTIAN ACTION

Several years ago in mid-December, my wife, Crickett, received a call from the mother of one of our daughter's friends. The mother's call was one of desperation—she was calling from the County Jail where she was being detained while awaiting a trial. She had been charged with Grand Theft Auto. The mother wanted us to post bail so she could get to her three children. Child Protective Services had placed the children with her disabled mother while her ex-husband was being located. According to the mother, her ex-husband was a dead-beat and was currently working offshore. When located, if he cared at all, he would most likely not return until after the New Year.

After a heartfelt, yet no nonsense, conversation, Crickett said "no" to making bail. But while on the phone and while looking me in the eyes, Crickett made an offer to the Mom. Before I tell you what the offer was, I need to go back to where Crickett was looking me in the eyes. Crickett and I have always approached issues in a unified manner. In this case, I was hearing only one side of the conversation, however, knowing Crickett's heart and our collective position on charitable action, there was no need for Crickett to consult me and there was no doubt in my mind what she was about to offer.

Back to the offer. Crickett offered that we take the three children into our home until which time she, the Mom, could make bail and come get her children or until which time the Father was contacted and could get their children in her absence.

The Mom took us up on our offer and we began to act. First, we contacted Child Protective Services just to give them a heads-up. Next, we called the grandmother. We wanted her buy-in and we got it. Then, my daughter got on the phone and invited her friend and the younger brother and sister to, as she put it; "spend the night for a while."

Six hours after saying "yes" to helping this family, we loaded up our three children and went to pick-up three more (9 years old, 4 years old and 18 months).

The dynamics of this undertaking required emergency planning, teamwork, problem solving, a whole lot of patience and a whole lot of prayer. Though we had no real idea as to how long we would have an extended family, we remained optimistic and made them feel welcome while never overlooking the fact that they (especially the oldest child) just had their lives turned upside down.

Over the course of their stay, everyone adapted to sleeping arrangements, bath schedules, house rules and coloring—lots of coloring. Crickett made several visits to the jail, each time taking current photos of the kids and news of their well being. Neighbors, church members and co-workers came to our assistance with clothes, Christmas gifts and many prayers.

What my family chose to do for the other family was based on our determined will (free will) to emulate Jesus and serve others while here on earth. We were centered in Christ and motivated by our love of God. What we did was to act like Christ. We fed, clothed and showed compassion to the needy. We took Christian Action.

The words Christian Action seem to define the phrase itself. *Christian—believing in Christ. Action—the manner or method of performing.* But where does Christian Action come from? What is its origin?

Christian Action—flows from a life in which Christ is centered and a life that is motivated by one's love for God.

There is a necessity for Christian Action in our lives if we plan to do what Christ asks of us in the book of Matthew; "You shall love God with all of your heart, all of your soul and with all of your mind...and..."You shall love your neighbor as you love yourself." It is God's intent to give us the very best there is, His Grace. Our human nature is such that we want to share with others the things we love and enjoy; things such as families, friends, hobbies and our work.

The spreading of Christian Action is accomplished through the gifts from the Holy Spirit. One gift in particular is that of charity. The others are equally as important when taking action as a Christian. You may want to refer back to the list of the gifts in Chapter 9.

We know we are uniquely gifted by means of the Holy Spirit. We also know that a life in grace, a life immersed in God's love, is achievable. So, if we take our God given talents, coupled with knowledge and understanding, and strive to remain in God's grace, the natural response is Christian Action.

For me, Christian Action is etched in my brain in the form of a simple, easy to recall, image. I imagine Christian Action as an arrow. This is fitting because like an arrow, Christian Action has an ultimate destination, a target if you will. That target is God's will.

The feather splices represent all the tools and skills gifted to us while we are Christ centered and motivated by love for God—all the value add measures that we addressed in previous chapters. Measures such as; knowledge, understanding, humility, patience, prayer and priorities.

The shaft of the arrow is a conduit between the means to take action and action itself. This is what overshadows us. It is what we live in when we are living right. It is God's Grace. Through His Grace, God is connecting the dots and creating opportunities where we can be in the position to help spread His good news.

The blunt or the blade of the arrow symbolize what actually flows from God's Grace, which is Christian Action.

My second eldest brother, who died at the age of 46, displayed Christian Action throughout his life. As his health deteriorated over the years, he was not as physically or financially able to do for others but he did what he could. I recall one Christmas when my Mom gave my brother a really nice shirt. When we were leaving my Mom's home later that afternoon, my brother was in front of me in his truck and I expected him to turn left toward his home. Instead he turned right. A week or two later, I asked him why he doesn't wear the shirt Mom gave him and he reluctantly told me that on Christmas Day he drove into town to a local Men's shelter called "Loaves and Fishes." After finding a man about his size sitting out front, my brother took the money he had in his own wallet, placed it in the shirt pocket and offered the shirt to the man in need.

Soon after this same brother of mine died, I found a kitchen check hidden away in his wallet on which he had written a poem or story. Though slightly humorous this story speaks volumes about what happens when we do not take action. My brother had titled what he wrote; "Whose Job Is It?"

This is a story about four people named Everybody, Somebody, Anybody and Nobody. There was an important job to be done and Everybody was sure Somebody would do it. Anybody could have done it, but Nobody did it. Somebody got angry about that because it was Everybody's job. Everybody thought Anybody could do it, but Nobody realized that Everybody wouldn't do it.

It ended up that Everybody blamed Somebody when Nobody did what Anybody could have done.

To me, my brother was playfully stating a fact. If you do not take the initiative, it's likely the intended act will never materialize. In terms of achieving God's will, that's not a good thing.

There are four Characteristics of Christian Action. The characteristics are:

Authenticity

Christian action is authentic. It is not self-serving. It is truly Christ-centered. We become motivated, enthusiastic, as a response to Christ's love for us and our love for Him.

Planning

A plan for Christian Action is essential. You should develop and nurture a solid relationship with a person before trying to introduce this friend to Christ. Set realistic goals based on your talents and gifts. It is a good idea to start small and add to your success.

Perseverance

You must Persevere. After starting your plan, follow it through to completion. Don't give up and leave everything to God and to others.

Balance

We must use our minds, our hearts and our hands to accomplish effective action. We must establish a comfortable balance between prayer and physical action. Christian Action does not act alone. We read in the book of Mark where "Jesus summoned the twelve and began to send them out two by two."**1**

Christian Action

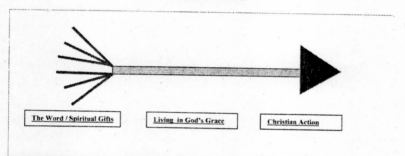

The Word / Spiritual Gifts   **Living in God's Grace**   **Christian Action**

Feather splices include things such as; Knowledge, Understanding, Humility, Patience,

Prayer, Priorities, etc.

Be sure to seek guidance through clergy, friends and prayer. Hitting your knees is a key component to hitting your goals.

Personally, I rely quite heavily on several dear friends; I referred to one in chapter 7 as my "Bible buddy." My friends in Christ are critical spokes in my spiritual wheel of Christian Action. One in particular is a religious Sister that God placed in my family's life years ago. This friend prays with me often. We focus on me not being as self serving, to not be as controlling (in a take charge, my way kind of way). We pray for me to plan, to preserver in and to balance my life in such a manner that it flows of Christian Action and perpetuates God's plan.

As mentioned in chapter 5 on Humility, I spent an extended period of time searching for a job following Crickett's and my decision to close a company we owned and operated for thirteen years. During that time, I had many opportunities to be authentic—authentically selfish, instead of selfless. I could have thrown process and planning out the door and traded perseverance in for pity and defeat. I could have justified imbalance and not used my mind, my heart and my hands to accomplish effective Christian Action.

During that very trying time, as leader of my family, I made a choice. After several bouts of denial and flat out being upset with the world and God, I made a choice. I chose to take up my Cross, take inventory of my talents, pray, set intermediate and long range goals and then, take action. Recall in chapter 7 of Discernment where I noted what Ann Steward said about purpose; "Its just waiting for you to tap into it and reverse the inertia into full drive."

During that time, my job was to find a job. But I also made it my job to serve others in the process. I cut the grass for several elderly people in our community. I teamed with others and built wheel chair ramps at the homes of those in need. I continued to teach CCD or Bible School. I say continued, because when classes started back up soon after us closing our company, I could have bowed out with several excuses. However, that particular year was a little different.

My oldest daughter, Shea, was going to be confirmed and I had been a Confirmation teacher at our Church for three consecutive years. How could I expect my daughter to truly be confirmed in her faith if I was not going to be a leading example of one persevering for the sake of righteousness despite the weight of my Cross?

I would regularly visit my Mom at an assisted living facility she eventually chose to move into after my Dad died. I often marveled at how she so selflessly displays Christian Action to her fellow residents. Mom would always open the door for the handicap residents before and after daily Mass at the on-site Chapel. Mom would say "I may not have a good mind any more but I have two good hands and two good legs."

Despite the perceived failures and any short comings in your life, you can still persevere and continue on with Christian Action. It's done by taking small steps in, with and through Christ toward a known and realistic goal.

In business, you often hear that success is all about location. Successful Christian Action is about you seeing and seizing an opportunity to bring a person closer to Christ. Successful Christian Action is making that person more aware of God's unconditional and abundant love.

The physical location or exact setting is not what seals the deal here. What you have to do is to know and love the person. You must remain confident and take action when the time feels right. The Holy Spirit will create the right environment and His power combined with your gifts will attract others to your joyful and optimistic demeanor— your Christ like demeanor. Soon those you feel compelled to show Christian Action towards will be emulating you and in many cases, working with you to serve others in kind.

I recently had an opportunity to take Christian Action and serve an ex-employee. I asked this friend to consider attending a ministry at our Church called "That Man Is You." I followed up my request with a personal letter and later sent a small prayer book along with an information sheet on the program. I earmarked several prayers and asked him to consider praying the prayers along with me for a week or so and to include the intentions of men like himself who were considering attending the program.

This friend not only attended 26 weekly sessions that started at 5:30 in the morning, he generally showed up at 4:30AM to help prepare the meeting room and assist the kitchen team with breakfast. Several times, he was sitting on the tailgate of his pick-up waiting on me to show up with the key.

In the opening of this chapter, I told you of the mother in jail and how she perceived her ex-husband as "deadbeat" and uncaring. Well…on day ten, the "Daddy" returned. I say Daddy because this is the endearing term his smiling and crying kids joyfully shouted as they ran into his open arms. He was a little leery of us at first, but when he noticed that we were not taking sides, just showing compassion, his guard lowered and the transition of his kids from our care to his went extremely well.

The mother made bail weeks later and trial was set for a few months out. Beyond that, to this day we have not heard from the family, but we pray for them often and we know that we penetrated their hearts through our Christian Action.

I thought it was fitting to close this chapter while speaking of Christian Action taken by The Virgin Mary—Jesus' Mom.

In the book of Luke it reads that Mary said; "Behold, I am the handmaid of the Lord. May it be done to me according to Your will." This is also known in Latin as Mary's "fiat." This is the equivalent to the words Christ spoke in the Lords Prayer—"Thy Will Be Done" that we discussed in Chapter one.

I said earlier that Christian Action is a natural response to God's grace. It was by the grace of God that the angle Gabriel was sent to announce Mary as the "favored one"—as His (God's) choice. This earthen vessel that would conceive in her womb, give birth to and help nurture for some thirty years, our Savior, Jesus Christ.

Mary's acceptance of God's will; Mary's selflessness; Mary's perseverance before, during and after her child's death are all hallmark examples of Christian Action. They each came as a result of God's grace. They came as a result of Mary living in God's grace.

We may never have Gabriel show up and point us out as God's favored ones. You know what, he doesn't have to. Jesus died for our sins and put us back in God's favor. If we just give our hearts to Christ through piety; if we just give our minds to Christ through study, we will remain in God's favor and we will be immersed in God's grace and we will naturally want to act—to say "Yes" to God's call...to God's will. I assure you, in doing this, we will successfully bring Christ into the world through our Christian Action.

The next time you have the opportunity to take Christian Action, please consider the words of Jesus' Mom spoken at the wedding feast in Cana; "Do whatever He tells you." 2

Chapter Twelve
FULL RELEASE

Chapter one of "Time Under the Cross" opened with a fearful and apprehensive statement toward surrendering of self and submitting to the power, authority and control of God. The statement was; "If I surrender, I will give up all that I have worked for, all that I have anguished over, all that I have dreamed to achieve." Though stated many years ago, there still remains the fear, in certain matters, where surrenderment or full release of my control, leaves me in an uncomfortable and compromising state of flux.

This occasional setback doesn't concern me as much as it did when I first began to understand and practice surrenderment. Now I feel better equipped to identify the driving force behind my fearful reluctance and through artful and prayerful application of the many gifts of the Holy Spirit, I am able to work in, with and through Jesus to restore my commitment and ability to achieve a full release from my control back to His.

It is my deepest prayer that "Time Under the Cross" has provided you with a few chinks of armor that will help fortify your ability to surrender to God while fending off the evil forces that never cease in their attempt to plant seeds of doubt, despair and denial into your mind and your heart. Furthermore, I pray that you see yourself as immersed in God's unconditional love and His radiant light while you live and serve with dominion as one created in God's own image and one who was chosen to spread His Good News.

I said at the close of chapter three on Understanding that I intended to take what I consider the requirements for surrenderment; enduring faith, mature sense of purpose and a determined will and break them down into bite size pieces throughout the remainder of the book. Also, I said that by the end of the book, hopefully we would have come full circle and would all have a strengthened awareness of what it takes to fully surrender to God.

Well, we are at the end of the book and this chapter, titled Full Release, culminates the process of surrenderment while accentuating the stabilizing fibers of surrender itself. I have selected twelve scripture references that I feel embody the essence of a disciplined Christian on his or her continuous journey to surrender all to God while still experiencing full joy through family, friends, church, work and recreation here on Earth.

Before we delve into the twelve scriptural passages that God put in my heart while I researched surrenderment, I would like to share with you why I titled this chapter "Full Release" instead of "Surrender."

The word "surrender" carries a negative connotation in my opinion yet it is the root of this book's central theme— Surrenderment. I wrote down and then scratched out the word "surrender" on the top of the first page of chapter twelve several times before I finally stopped and prayed the prayer I mentioned in chapter two that I use when I begin to feel overwhelmed. "God I'm doing it again. Please give me the wisdom to surrender what is weighting me down here and free my mind so that I can discern, choose and move on." Seconds later, I visualized myself preparing to go fishing as I often do.

Fishing is one of my favorite hobbies and an excellent way for me to spend some quiet time with God while taking in the natural beauty of His creation. One of the priorities in my preparation for a fishing trip is to catch live bait in the Laguna Madre (Mother Lagoon) near Padre Island along the Texas Gulf Coast. I visualized myself making the perfect cast with my throw net. If you have never used a throw net, it requires much practice and the perfect cast is one where the net is opened to its designed maximum diameter and the draw rope is completely uncoiled allowing the net to travel the full length of the rope without yanking your shoulder out of joint and prematurely closing the net. That is assuming you remembered to attach the draw rope to your wrist in the first place.

The most vital step in the process behind achieving the perfect cast is a "Full Release."

Just like with the perfect cast, surrenderment requires knowledge, practice and a full release. We must trust Jesus with and in everything. We must let go of our control, despite our wants, fears and perceived rights. When we do this, we will experience the exhilaration of knowing that what we released is in God's capable and loving hands. When we do this, we will reap many gifts and produce much fruit as a result of our faith and belief in Him. "After He had finished speaking, He (Jesus) said to Simon, 'put out into deep water and lower your nets for a catch' ... When they had done this, they caught a great number of fish and their nets were tearing."
1

The twelve scriptural passages I mentioned above are all from various books in the New Testament. They each contain a message pertaining to surrendering and fully releasing self to God's Divine power and plan. Each message is intended for you personally and each has been written for you to hear with your heart, right here and right now.

I suggest you use the form or style of prayer mentioned in chapter eight; *Lectio Divina (Sacred Readings)* where you slowly read the scripture passage several times, if necessary, while listening for what it is saying to you. Let God's Word soak into your heart and know that He is with you this very moment.

Jesus in the desert—"Get away, Satan! It is written: 'The Lord, your God, shall you worship and Him alone shall you serve.'" **Matthew 4:10**

"While the crowd was pressing in on Jesus and listening to the word of God, He was standing by the Lake of Gennesaret. He saw two boats there alongside the lake; the fishermen had disembarked and were washing their nets. Getting into one of the boats, the one belonging to Simon, He asked him to put out a short distance from the shore. Then He sat down and taught the crowds from the boat. After He had finished speaking, He said to Simon, 'Put out into deep water and lower your nets for a catch.' Simon said in reply, 'Master, we have worked hard all night and have caught nothing, but at Your command I will lower the nets.' When they had done this, they caught a great number of fish and their nets were tearing. They signaled to their partners in the other boat to come to help them. They came and filled both boats so that they were in danger of sinking. When Simon Peter saw this, he fell at the knees of Jesus and said, 'Depart from me, Lord, for I am a sinful man.' For astonishment at the catch of fish they had made seized him and all those with him, and likewise James and John, the sons of Zebedee, who were partners of Simon. Jesus said to Simon, 'Do not be afraid; from now on you will be catching men.' When they brought their boats to the shore, they left everything [2] and followed Him." **Luke 5:1-11**

"If anyone wishes to come after Me, he must deny himself and take up his cross daily and follow Me." **Luke 9:23**

John the Baptist responding to his disciples—"He must increase; I must decrease." **John 3:30**

"I am the vine, you are the branches. Whoever remains in Me and I in him will bear much fruit, because without Me you can do nothing." **John 15:5**

St. Paul speaking—"…yet I live, no longer I, but Christ lives in me; insofar as I now live in the flesh, I live by faith in the Son of God who has loved me and given Himself up for me." **Galatians 2:20**

St. Paul speaking—"be filled with the Spirit, addressing one another (in) psalms and hymns and spiritual songs, singing and playing to the Lord in your hearts, giving thanks always and for everything in the name of our Lord Jesus Christ to God the Father. Be subordinate to one another out of reverence for Christ." **Ephesians 5:18-21**

St. Paul speaking—"It is not that I have already taken hold of it or have already attained perfect maturity, but I continue my pursuit in hope that I may possess it, since I have indeed been taken possession of by Christ (Jesus). Brothers, I for my part do not consider myself to have taken possession. Just one thing: forgetting what lies behind but straining forward to what lies ahead, I continue my pursuit toward the goal, the prize of God's upward calling, in Christ Jesus." **Philippians 3:12-14**

St. Paul speaking—"Persevere in prayer, being watchful in it with thanksgiving."

"Let your speech always be gracious, seasoned with salt, so that you know how you should respond to each one." **Colossians 4:2, 6**

"So submit yourselves to God. Resist the devil, and he will flee from you. Draw near to God, and He will draw near to you. Cleanse your hands, you sinners, and purify your hearts, you of two minds." **James 4:7-8**

Above all, let your love for one another be intense, because love covers a multitude of sins. Be hospitable to one another without complaining. As each one has received a gift, use it to serve one another as good stewards of God's varied grace. Whoever preaches, let it be with the words of God; whoever serves, let it be with the strength that God supplies, so that in all things God may be glorified through Jesus Christ." **1 Peter 4:8-11**

"And all of you, clothe yourselves with humility in your dealings with one another, for: 'God opposes the proud but bestows favor on the humble.' So humble yourselves under the mighty hand of God, that He may exalt you in due time. Cast all your worries upon Him because he cares for you." **1 Peter 5:5-7**

I wish to thank each of you for opening your hearts and allowing God in. Also, I want to thank you for allowing me to share my own trials, triumphs and attempts at surrenderment. I am no different than others trying to follow Christ. I too am simply a sinner in rehab.

Please join me in the following prayer written by my Bible buddy I mentioned in chapter seven on Discernment. I asked him to write what came to his heart as a closing prayer for "Time Under the Cross."

My dear Sweet and Patient Lord as You know, I have placed my big toe into the cold waters of surrenderment many times. The ripple I have made is almost unnoticeable. Please bless me with the strength of the Holy Spirit to just dive in and let His love lead me to where it is You want me to go. Wash away all my fears as I swim out to deep water; water which can consume me, but instead will be waters of a new Baptism in unity and fellowship with You. I ask for this and all Your gifts in the name of Jesus Christ, my Savior. Amen.

NOTES

All Bible references are from the New American Bible unless specifically noted otherwise.

Chapter One

   1 2 Samuels 22:2
   2 Matthew 6:9-13 and Luke 11:2-4
   3 Genesis 1:27-28
   4 Matthew 22: 37-39
   5 James 1:12 *(Emphasis mine)*
   6 John 8:32—Darby Bible Translation
   7 How to Pray the Rosary, www.rosary-center.org

Chapter Two

   1 Benjamin Bloom - Bloom's Taxonomy of Educational Objectives.
   2 Nancy M. Dixon. Common Knowledge: How Companies Thrive by Sharing What They Know (Boston: Harvard Business School Press, 2000), p. 13
   3 Thomas H. Davenport and Laurence Prusak, Working Knowledge: How Organizations Manage What They Know (Boston: Harvard Business School Press, 1998), p. 5
   4 "Knowledge"—Baker's Evangelical Dictionary of Biblical Theology—Crosswalk.com
   5 Faith Publishing House, *Evening Light Songs*, 1949, edited 1987, p.504

6 Matthew 4:1,10
7 Col. 1:17
8 1 John 5:11
9 Matthew 6:19
10 Isaiah 53:12
11 John 1:17-18
12 John 17:3
13 Job 33:14
14 Exodus 31:3
15 Quote—Mother of one of my dear friends. Mrs. Flores and her husband are Ranchers and Christians and live just outside of Concepcion, Texas. Lovely people.

Chapter Three

1 www.acts17-11.com—Bible Studies—"Knowledge" p. 5-6
2 1 Corinthians 12:8, 28
3 This technique was originally developed by Sakichi Toyoda and was adopted by Toyota Motor Corporation during the evolution of Toyota's manufacturing methodologies. To quote Taiichi Ohno, the architect of the Toyota Production System; "…by repeating why five times, the nature of the problem as well as its solution becomes clear." This tool has seen widespread use beyond Toyota, and is now also used within Six Sigma.
4 James 1:5

Chapter Four

1 Hebrews 10:35-36 & 11:1
2 Hebrews 11:6
3 Matthew 14:28 "Take courage, it is I; don't be afraid"

4 Stuart McAllister, Vice President of Training and Special Projects—Ravi Zacharias International Ministries
5 Matthew 24:12-13 (emphasis is mine)
6 Matthew 27:16
7 Hebrews 3:18
8 1 Corinthians 10:13

Chapter Five

1 Arrogate—To claim or seize without justification as one's right. (Meriam Webster Dictionary)
2 In the time of the first century, Christians were being killed quite vigorously by the Romans. St. Paul or Saul was a highly decorated and proven advocate of this edict before his conversion on the road to Damascus.
3 Matthew 5:5-7, 9, 10
4 Matthew 5:5-7, 9-10
5 Easton's Bible Dictionary—Search; "Humility"
6 Source/Author Unknown
7 1Samuel 13:14 (emphasis mine)
8 Job 1:18
9 John 15:1-2

Chapter Six

1 Exodus 32:9-10
2 Exodus 32:11
3 Exodus 32:14
4 Exodus 32:15
5 Mark 6:7
6 Mark 6:35
7 Matthew 14:17
8 John 15:13

9 Romans 15:4 GNT

10 James 1:2-3

11 John 14:6—"Jesus said to him, "I am **the way** and the truth and the life. No one comes to the Father except through me."

Chapter Seven

1 Revelations 3:16

2 Mark 1:13

3 Matthew 14:23

4 Mark 1:13

5 Matthew 21:17

6 Matthew 26:44 (emphasis mine) & Matthew 26:42

7 Luke 2:46 (emphasis mine) & Luke 2:51-52

8 John 1:14

9 Romans 12:2

Chapter Eight

1 In 1791, Isaac Collins and Isaiah Thomas respectively produced the first family Bible and first illustrated Bible printed in America. Both were King James Versions. (www.greatsite.com)— English Bible History Section—

2 Article—"Exploring a Life of Prayer" (1990) written by Rev. Vennard

3 John 9:31

4 Definition from Dictionary.com Unabridged V1.1

5 Matthew 7:7

6 Colossians 4:2

7 Catholic Encyclopedia: Prayer; p. 4—www.newadvent.org

8 Thessalonians 5:17

9 Mark 13:33

10 Ephesians 6:11
11 Matthew 18:20

Chapter Nine

1 John 15:9 NAS
2 Galatians 5:22-23; "...the fruit of the Spirit is love, joy, peace, patience, kindness, generosity, faithfulness, gentleness, self-control."
3 Deuteronomy 5:6-7
4 Deuteronomy 5:11
5 Deuteronomy 5:12
6 Mark 12:30
7 Mark 12:31
8 Acts 20:35
9 **Time**—Psalm 31:15, Ephesians 5:15-16, Matthew 6:33 **Talents**—Exodus 36:1, Eccl. 9:10, Colossians 3:23-24, 1 Corin. 12:7-9, 1 Corin. 12:27, 1 Peter 4:10 **Treasure**—1 Chron. 29:11, Luke 16:11, Matthew 6:21, Colossians 3:2, Hebrews 13:5
10 Matthew 5:15
11 Luke 4:42-43

Chapter Ten

1 John 12:24
2 James 1:2-3
3 Ephesians 5:18
4 "When all hostility, resentment, fear and insecurities are erased from your mind, the state that remains is pure joy. When we become established in that state, we live in joy always." Eknath Easwaran's Book—Original Goodness (Copyright 1996—The Blue Mountain Center of Meditation)
5 Matthew 19:26

6 "Gifts of the Holy Spirt," Article by Fr. Michael Champagne, Feb. 1998

7 Long Suffering is also referred to as longanimity, forbearance and most commonly as patience throughout the New Testament.

8 www.wikipedia.org—Search word(s); Joyful, Joyful We Adore Thee

9 Psychology—The Search for Understanding by Janet a. Simons,

10 Donald B. Irwin and Beverly A. Drinnien. West Publishing Company,

11 New York, 1987

Chapter Eleven

1 Mark 6:7
2 John 2:5

Chapter Twelve

1 Luke 5:4, 6